Introducing Communication

INTRODUCING COMMUNICATION

PERSPECTIVES, ASSUMPTIONS, AND IMPLICATIONS

Amardo Rodriguez

UNIVERSITY OF TORONTO PRESS
Toronto Buffalo London

© University of Toronto Press 2020
Toronto Buffalo London
utorontopress.com
Printed in Canada

ISBN 978-1-4875-0714-5 (cloth)   ISBN 978-1-4875-3566-7 (EPUB)
ISBN 978-1-4875-2482-1 (paper)   ISBN 978-1-4875-3565-0 (PDF)

Library and Archives Canada Cataloguing in Publication

Title: Introducing communication : perspectives, assumptions, and implications / Amardo Rodriguez.
Names: Rodriguez, Amardo, author.
Description: Includes bibliographical references and index.
Identifiers: Canadiana (print) 2019020639X | Canadiana (ebook) 2019020642X
    | ISBN 9781487507145 (cloth) | ISBN 9781487524821 (paper) | ISBN 9781487535650 (PDF)
    | ISBN 9781487535667 (EPUB)
Subjects: LCSH: Communication.
Classification: LCC P90 .R63 2020 | DDC 302.23—dc23

We welcome comments and suggestions regarding any aspect of our publications—please feel free to contact us at news@utorontopress.com or visit us at utorontopress.com.

Every effort has been made to contact copyright holders; in the event of an error or omission, please notify the publisher.

University of Toronto Press acknowledges the financial assistance to its publishing program of the Canada Council for the Arts and the Ontario Arts Council, an agency of the Government of Ontario.

Canada Council   Conseil des Arts
for the Arts   du Canada

Funded by the   Financé par le
Government   gouvernement
of Canada   du Canada   Canadä

*For
Joshua and Jordan*

Of all things, communication is the most wonderful.

John Dewey

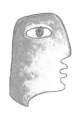

CONTENTS

FIGURES

The study of communication is one of the most complex and difficult tasks ever undertaken by mankind.

Dennis Smith and L. Keith Williamson

PROLOGUE

This book organizes and introduces different perspectives to studying, theorizing, and understanding communication. It highlights the assumptions that guide these different perspectives, as well as the ethical, political, and epistemological implications and consequences that flow from each of them. Together, these different communication perspectives reveal that studying communication is important, and this diversity of perspectives enriches the study of communication by showcasing the power of communication to make a better world, and even the integral role that communication *must* play in any mission to create a just and humane world. For what is all but certain is that there can be no better world without better communication.

The goal of this book is to be pedagogically profound as regards revealing why the study of communication is important in terms of deepening our understanding of the human condition, enlarging how we frame and resolve human problems and struggles, and appreciating the different perspectives that communication brings to the study of the human experience. Indeed, the study of communication is important because we create ourselves, each other, and our worlds through communication. How we communicate will determine what becomes of us and our worlds. In other words, how we define and experience communication will determine what becomes possible. Communication is the womb of possibility. The study of communication is important because the consequences of communication are important. Communication is not only the most *difficult* thing we have ever sought to understand, but also the most *important* thing we have ever sought to understand.

This book highlights the consequences and implications that come with different ways of defining, understanding, and studying communication. Its goal is to promote a robust and rigorous examination of these different consequences and implications, and also to encourage us to look reflectively on how these consequences and implications affect us. We understand the importance of communication by appreciating the importance and substance of these consequences and implications.

After presenting the different perspectives to studying, theorizing, and understanding communication, the book introduces and discusses various issues that are increasingly impacting and even disrupting the practice of communication, regardless of one's perspective. These issues, among others, deal with the continuing rise of various political and social movements that aim to limit communication in the name of promoting civility, decency, and diversity; an increasing effort by many governments and religious regimes to also limit communication by enacting blasphemy and heresy laws; a heightening hostility and proclivity for war as the world's natural resources diminish; the altering of our communication behaviors as a result of new kinds of technology increasingly penetrating our lives; and the continuing challenge to the civilizational and epistemological hegemony in communication studies from people from various corners of the world. These are no doubt difficult and challenging times for the world. However, at the core of this book is the belief that the study of communication is important because communication is our only path to an enduring peace and prosperity.

This book presents an introduction to these different perspectives. It focuses on how each perspective defines communication and also approaches the study of communication. It also unpacks the different ethics and politics that surround each perspective. Ultimately, this book highlights the contribution that each perspective offers to the study of communication and adds to the diversity and plurality in communication studies.

I designed this book for people who believe that teaching and learning should be about promoting discussion, deliberation, and reflection. It will especially appeal to those who believe that we only learn anything profound by rigorously challenging and questioning what we value and believe. In this case, this book aspires to challenge what we commonly value and believe about communication, to examine how we engage with and experience communication, and to invite us to explore new ways of defining and experiencing communication that make for better outcomes. Its goal is to make us wise about communication. Being wise is about being able to look honestly and rigorously at the consequences of our actions, and knowing what actions make for what consequences. In this regard, wisdom is about being able to look into the future. What consequences will come from our actions or lack thereof? How will our actions—in this case our communication actions and decisions—lead to different outcomes?

DIFFERENT PERSPECTIVES
IN COMMUNICATION STUDIES

The primary goal of this book is to introduce the dominant perspectives that constitute the study and practice of communication in the Western/European world. As Stephen W. Littlejohn (1996), author of one of the most popular textbooks in communication studies, *Theories of Human Communication*, reminds us, "The study of communication as we have understood it in the United States and in Europe is a Western, Eurocentric endeavor. Virtually all [our theories] come from the Western academic tradition" (pp. 4–5). However, as much as this is the case, in this book I introduce many issues and concepts from outside the Western/European world. These issues and concepts enrich our understanding of communication in many important ways. In fact, these issues and concepts highlight the fact that nearly all civilizations take the study of communication seriously and possess understandings of communication that can be valuable to all of us. Finally, inclusion of these issues and concepts reminds us that our new world is a plural and multicultural world, and the study of communication needs to begin to reflect this reality.

I organize the different communication perspectives under the following headings: Communication as *Language and Symbols*, Communication as *Messages*, Communication as *Media*, Communication as *Meanings*, Communication as *Narratives*, Communication as *Performances*, Communication as *Relationships*, and, finally, Communication as *Modes of Being*. The objectives of this book are (1) to recognize the core assumptions shaping, framing, and situating these different perspectives to the study and practice of communication and the civilizational (worldview) origins of these assumptions;

(2) to appreciate the social, ethical, political, and theoretical implications and limitations that come with these different perspectives; (3) to describe and advocate for the conceptual and ideological diversity that comes with these different perspectives; (4) to promote and encourage asking new questions that can potentially expand and enrich our understanding of communication; and, finally, (5) to recognize and appreciate the issues, struggles, and challenges that face the study and practice of communication locally and globally.

In my discussion and presentation of all the different perspectives on communication, the goal is to present a rigorous understanding of how communication shapes our lives and our social worlds. I come to the study of communication from the standpoint that communication is *constitutive*—through communication we create and manage our social, personal, political, and cultural worlds. In the words of Steve Duck and David McMahan (2017), authors of *Communication in Everyday Life*, communication "creates the stuff of life." Through communication we create identities, ethnicities, sexualities, realities, and possibilities. All of these things are also "maintained, negotiated, challenged, and altered through communication." For Lee Thayer (1974), "No one of us is born human; we must be made human. It is in and through communication that we individually emerge as human beings. We come into this world knowing almost nothing of what we will need to know to live in it. All knowledge must be learned; and it must be learned in and through communication" (p. 1). For Deanna Fassett, John Warren, and Keith Nainby (2018), authors of *Communication: A Critical/Cultural Introduction*, "Understanding communication as constitutive means exploring how communication works to create, understand, and challenge power and privilege, oppression, and justice" (p. 18). That communication is constitutive means that the study of communication helps us understand how best to shape, navigate, and organize our different social worlds, including all the struggles and challenges that come with such worlds. It also means that the study of communication is about understanding the communication forces and experiences that shape our view of ourselves, and that the study of communication is ultimately about understanding the limits of what we view as possible. That is, how can we create new ways of defining and experiencing communication that make better worlds possible?

chapter one

COMMUNICATION AS LANGUAGE AND SYMBOLS

I

To view communication from the perspective of language and symbols is to believe that human beings are fundamentally symbolic and linguistic beings, and that our linguistic and symbolic capacity is responsible for our evolutionary prosperity and superiority. Human beings, claims Kenneth Burke (1989), are a "symbol-using, symbol-making, and symbol-misusing animal" (p. 60). We create symbols to name things and situations, to relate to other human beings and things, and to manipulate and take advantage of others. For Mark Redmond (2015), "Symbols are probably the single most important quality that gives us our humanness, separating us from all other animals. Without symbols no other human creation is possible. Symbols allow us to remember and reminisce, to evaluate and plan, to coordinate, to communicate abstract thoughts, to think about the future, and to consider alternatives and outcomes." James W. Neuliep (2015), author of *Intercultural Communication: A Contextual Approach*, writes, "Human communication—that is, the ability to symbolize and use language—separates humans from animals. Communication with others is the essence of what it means to be human" (p. 10). George Gerbner (1974) claims that "communication is the chief distinguishing mark and evolutionary force of our species." It is why "homo sapiens emerged from the ice age accomplished artists, scientists, and organizers" (p. 58). For Joel Charon, "It is the symbol that translates the world from the physical sensed reality to a reality that can be understood, dissected, integrated, and tested.

Between reality and what we see and do stands the symbol. Once we learn symbols we are in a position of understanding our environment rather than simply responding to it, and once that happens what we come to see and act on is colored by our symbols" (quoted in Redmond, 2015).

In a paper titled *Is Language Unique to Human Species?*, Ulla Hedeager (2011) writes, "Language, being an efficient human adaptation to the environment, evolved by natural selection. This seems indeed the most likely scientific explanation, and unless we believe in a divine origin, there should be no reason to reject a Darwinian point of view" (p. 2). We are to assume that without symbols, there would be no sciences, no religions, no moral, cultural, political, or educational systems. Language is supposedly responsible for us being a superior species. For James W. Carey (2009), "Communication is a symbolic process whereby reality is produced, maintained, repaired, and transformed" (p. 8). It also makes for "the ambience of human existence" (p. 9). For C. David Mortensen (1991), "language, conflict, and communication initially arose from pressures built in to the critical life-or-death situations our ancestors were compelled to share with one another" (p. 275). In other words, the demands of evolution, such as finding better means of getting along and working with others to achieve common goals, supposedly made for the rise of language and communication. According to Daniel Dennett (1994), director for the Center for Cognitive Studies at Tufts University, "We human beings may not be the most admirable species on the planet, or the most likely to survive another millennium, but we are without any doubt at all the most intelligent. We are also the only species with language" (p. 161). In *Descent of Man*, Charles Darwin (1871) said that "articulate language was ... peculiar to man" (p. 54).

For Byron Reese (2018), author of *The Fourth Age: Smart Robots, Conscious Computers, and the Future of Humanity*, "Language came about because of our bigger brains, and in a virtuous cycle, language in turn grew our brains even bigger, as there are kinds of thoughts we cannot think without words. Words are symbols, after all, and we can combine and alter those ideas in ways that are inconceivable without the technology of speech" (p. 11). Reese believes that the rise of language was vital to our survival as a species. Besides allowing us to exchange information, "language enabled us to cooperate with each other, which is one of our singular abilities as a species. Without language, a dozen people were no match for a wooly mammoth. But with language, those people could work together in a way that made them nearly invincible" (pp. 10–11). However, the problem with this hugely popular evolutionary story about the origins of language and communication is that linguists and anthropologists have never found a pre-evolved language, meaning a language that is inherently inferior to others. Even Reese acknowledges this fact. Grammatically, conceptually, and structurally, all languages are fully formed, equally capable of allowing us to process complex thought. No language is inherently inferior to another.

In *The First Idea: How Symbols, Language, and Intelligence Evolved from Our Primate Ancestors to Modern Humans*, Stanley Greenspan and Stuart Shanker (2004) reject the commonly held view that natural selection forces made for the rise of language and communication. To begin with, claim Greenspan and Shanker, there is no evidence "that genes by themselves ... can explain complex interactive behavior, problem solving, or thinking" (p. 39). It is instead the ability to learn "that enabled human beings to engage in interactive learning experiences and to acquire tools of learning, including emotional signals, problem-solving capacities, and the use of symbols to organize and reflect on experience" (p. 39). Greenspan and Shanker contend that this kind of learning is passed down culturally rather than biologically. In other words, this kind of learning requires "nurturing practices that must be provided anew for each new generation.... Although our potential for learning is genetically mediated, the development of emotional signaling, problem solving, symbol formation, and reflective thinking, that is, our intelligence, is a culturally dependent process" (p. 40). That these practices are culturally dependent means that our minds are always culturally situated. It also means that the workings of our minds and our capacity to learn can always be improved by improving the conditions found in cultural environments.

Noam Chomsky, arguably the most important linguist of the last century, also rejects the natural selection account on the origins of language and communication. Chomsky contends that language is uniquely human, meaning that all human beings have the same language program. In other words, all languages equally possess the capacity to create and share complex thought. Language diversity has nothing to do with languages being superior or inferior. Those distinctions are purely of our making, to justify our belief that certain peoples are superior to others. A **dialect** is merely a language of people who are without power and status. Nothing about any dialect is linguistically deficient. Suffice it to say, Chomsky forcefully rejects the natural selection story/theory on the origin of language. Chomsky claims that human beings are uniquely programmed and equipped for language. In *Language and Mind*, Chomsky (2006) writes, "Anyone concerned with the study of human nature and human capacities must somehow come to grips with the fact that all normal human beings acquire language ... human language appears to be uniquely human" (p. 59). Chomsky contends all languages follow a fixed set of universal principles of language structure that are biologically determined. As a result, language differences are cultural rather than biological, meaning that no language is inherently inferior to another.

According to Chomsky, "My own work leads me to the conclusion that ... language structures are uniform. The uniformity results from the existence of fixed, immutable, biologically determined principles, which provide the schematism which makes a child capable of organizing and coming to terms with his rather restricted experiences of everyday life and creating complex intellectual structures on that basis" (pp. 151–52). Chomsky labels this natural algorithm a Universal Grammar. Universal Grammar is an example of what biologists call a strange attractor—a self-organizing force found in all living systems. Strange attractors allow any naturally occurring system to take on endless possible variations and expressions. According to Chomsky, "I think in a general way we can say that a person's knowledge of his language is based on a system of rules and principles. If you look carefully at these rules, you will discover that the rules themselves are of a narrow range. There are certain kinds of rules that are permissible; there are other kinds of rules that are not permissible. There are also strict conditions on their application" (p. 152). In short, no language is less complex than others. Still, the commonly held belief that our own evolution as a species correlates with the evolution of language is at the core of the notion that certain languages are superior to other languages, and, consequently, civilizations with supposedly superior languages are inherently superior to civilizations with supposedly inferior languages.

This false assumption remains the foundation for arguments that claim various peoples (races) are inherently (biologically) superior to others. The assumption appears this way in Charles Darwin's (1871) *The Descent of Man*, "No doubt, the difference in this respect is enormous, even if we compare the mind of one of the lowest savages, who has no words to express any number higher than four, and who uses no abstract terms for the commonest objects or affections, with that of the most highly organized ape" (p. 34).

This assumption also appears in an 1887 annual report by the United States Commissioner of Indian Affairs: "Teaching an Indian youth in his own barbarous dialect is a positive detriment to him. The impracticability, if not impossibility, of civilizing the Indians of this country in any other tongue than our own would seem obvious" (Chamberlin, 2003, p. 18). The assumption can also be found in a popular segregation book by Thomas Pickens Brady (1954) titled *Black Monday: Segregation or Amalgamation*: "The negro could not be expected to participate in the conquest of these United States. His language consisted mostly, at the time of the Revolutionary War, of grunts, a sign language and a few words. The jargon of the jungle was in his tongue and the Congo flowed deep in his brain. He was being taught and was learning words sufficient in his new language to make known his wants" (p. 12). The assumption also pervades Alvin Schmidt's (1997) book *The Menace of Multiculturalism*: "English, like no other language, has been the medium by which the British and their descendants, the Americans, fashioned a culture of freedom and liberty that other societies with different languages have not even come close to equaling.... The world's greatest articles and documents of human rights and freedom were first written in the English language.... Without being a linguistic determinist, one is nevertheless moved to ask: Why has no other language inspired such monumental hallmarks of freedom?" (pp. 122–23).

Then there is the social brain hypothesis, which claims that the evolutionary need for communication systems to manage the demands and tensions of complex social relationships is responsible for the superior size of our brains and also the increasing capacity of our brains. Robin Dunbar (2002), professor of evolutionary psychology and behavioral ecology at the University of Liverpool, states, "There is ample evidence that primate social systems are more complex than those of other species. These systems can be shown to involve processes such as tactical deception and coalition formation, which are rare or occur in simpler forms in other taxonomic groups" (p. 69). Dunbar contends that our superior communication capacity can be seen in the metaphorical nature of language. Dunbar writes, "a great deal of linguistic communication is based in metaphor. Understanding the intentions behind a metaphor is crucial to successful communication. Failure to understand these intentions commonly results in confusion or inappropriate responses. Indeed, without these abilities it is doubtful whether literature, notably poetry, would be possible. Our conversations would be confined to the banal factual" (pp. 84–85). However, Dunbar gives us no account of the origins of our own highly complex social system that, in turn, supposedly makes for our superior communication facility that, in turn, supposedly made for our superior brain size. In short, how exactly did our superior complex system initially come about to now need a superior communication facility and superior brain to give birth to this facility?

In the end, no language is inherently superior or inferior to any other language. The popular notion that languages reflect superior/inferior peoples, cultures, and civilizations has no foundation in science or history. It is a myth, a falsehood. The popular notion that the quality of one's language reflects the quality of one's mind (e.g., a large vocabulary or early mastery of language reflects a superior mind) also has no foundation in science or history. This is also a myth, a falsehood. Finally, the popular notion that languages need the imposition of human rules to be coherent, and that without such rules (e.g., subject/verb agreement, no splitting of infinitives) communication will be impossible also has no foundation in science or history. It is a myth, a falsehood. In the end, how we use language is much more important than what kind of language we use. Do we, for instance, use language to heal or harm, to understand or condemn, to unite or divide, to love or hate?

II

To view communication from the perspective of language and symbols is to believe that what distinguishes us from other species is our supposedly superior linguistic and symbolic capacity. In a famous speech titled *Antidosis*, Isocrates said that "because there has been implanted in us the power to persuade each other and to make clear to each other whatever we desire, not only have we escaped the life of wild beasts, but we have come together and founded cities and made laws and invented arts; and, generally speaking, there is no institution devised by man which the power of speech has not helped us to establish" (Jasinski, 2001, p. xiv). Sam Harris (2010), author of *The Moral Landscape: How Science Can Determine Human Values*, claims that the rise of language gave our ancestors the ability to gradually displace and physically eradicate "all rivals." For Harris, "there is no question that syntactic language lies at the root of our ability to understand the universe, to communicate ideas, to cooperate with another in complex societies, and to build (one hopes) a sustainable, global civilization" (pp. 114–15). He goes on to contend that "the power of language surely results from the fact that it allows mere words to substitute for direct experience and mere thoughts to simulate possible states of the world" (p. 115). Similarly, Scott Russell Sanders (2000) writes, "language is our distinguishing gift, our hallmark as a species" (p. 86). For Jess Alberts, Thomas Nakayama, and Judith Martin (2007), authors of *Human Communication in Society*, "Symbolic communication is uniquely human. When animals communicate they typically use iconic and indexical messages, but rarely do they understand symbolic communication, except when taught by humans. For example, a person can teach a dog certain words (fetch, treat, walk), but a dog cannot teach another dog what these words mean" (p. 11).

In *Communication in the Real World*, a communication textbook by Richard Jones, Jr. (2017), the story appears this way: "Even though all animals communicate, human beings have a special capacity to use symbols to communicate about things outside our immediate temporal and spatial reality. For example, we have the capacity to use abstract symbols, like the word education, to discuss a concept that encapsulates many aspects of teaching and learning. We can also reflect on the past and imagine our future. The ability to think outside our immediate reality is what allows us to create elaborate belief systems, art, philosophy, and academic theories. It's true that you can teach a gorilla to sign words like food and baby, but its ability to use symbols doesn't extend to the same level of abstraction as ours." For Stephen Littlejohn (1996), "The ability to communicate on a higher level separates humans from other animals" (p. 3).

In *Language and Human Behavior*, Derek Bickerton (1995) writes, "The claim that we are just another species ignores the range as well as the power of human behavior. The range of behavior in other creatures does not extend much beyond seeking food, seeking sex, rearing and protecting young, resisting predation, grooming, fighting rivals, exploring and defending territory, and unstructured play. Human beings do all these things, of course, but they also do math, tap dance, engage in commerce, build boats, play chess, invent novel artifacts, drive vehicles, litigate, draw representationally, and do countless other things that no other species ever did. As such, any theory that would account for human behavior has to explain why the behavior of all other species is, relatively speaking, so limited, while that of one single species should be so broad. Why is there not a continuum of behaviors, grow-ing gradually from amoeba to human? Why don't chimpanzees build boats, why can't orangutans tap dance?" (p. 6). It is supposedly our superior lin-guistic and symbolic capacity that allows us to rule the world, which suppos-edly emerged from evolutionary forces and pressures that made our survival dependent on creating new kinds of coordination and organization that in-volved better modes of communication.

Writing in the *New York Review of Books*, Steven Mithen (2015) describes the evolution of language as "a unique evolutionary development" that oc-curred "a mere 100,000 years ago within a single lineage of apes somewhere in Africa." According to Mithen, "This was not merely a more complex form of vocal and gestural communication that all apes possess, one that reached its apogee with the Neanderthals. Language was the vehicle for a new type of thought that provided *Homo sapiens* with their competitive edge over all other species as they dispersed from Africa 70,000 years ago. The use of language created a new dynamic of culture change. In a tiny, very recent moment of evolutionary time, *Homo sapiens*, the only language-using ape, has created re-markable works of art and scientific achievement." In *The Origins of Political Order*, Francis Fukuyama (2011) claims that the "emergence of language among early human beings opened up huge new opportunities for both im-proved cooperation and cognitive development in an intimately linked fash-ion. Having language means that knowledge of who was honest and who [was] deceitful no longer depends on direct experience, but can be passed on to others as social knowledge" (p. 35). Moreover, according to Fukuyama, the development of language opened "the possibility of abstraction and theory, critical cognitive faculties that are unique to human beings. Words can refer to concrete objects as well as to abstract classes of objects (dogs, trees) and to ab-stractions that refer to invisible forces (Zeus, gravity). Putting the two together makes possible mental models—that is, general statements about causation. All human beings engage in the construction of abstract mental models; our ability to theorize in this fashion gives us huge survival advantages" (p. 36).

However, if language does make us cognitively superior to other species, what are we to make of members of different species achieving deep and caring relationships (such as an elephant and a dog, a deer and a lion, a mon-key and a tiger) without sharing a common linguistic and symbolic system? Many of these relationships between different species are documented in

Jennifer Holland's *Unlikely Friendships: 47 Remarkable Stories from the Animal Kingdom* (2011) and *Unlikely Loves: 43 Heartwarming True Stories from the Animal Kingdom* (2013). Also, what other species has put the planet in such ecological peril? Moreover, what other species has a history that includes slavery and the Holocaust? For instance, when did dogs ever enslave other dogs, or wage war on other dogs? When did dogs ever engage in genocide? Further, although other species may seemingly lack a linguistic and symbolic system comparable to ours, why must we take this to mean that they possess an inferior communication capacity? Indeed, why should other species be measured by our own definition of communication? Also, where is the evidence that our supposed superior linguistic and symbolic system has made us morally and intellectually superior to other species? Simply put, where is the evidence that our supposedly superior linguistic and symbolic system has made our lives richer and better than that of other species?

III

To view communication from the perspective of language and symbols is to believe that communication is fundamentally a linguistic and symbolic phenomenon. The study of communication from this perspective is about how to use language and symbols effectively, appropriately, and persuasively, meaning how to use language and symbols to achieve our goals and objectives. Indeed, to view communication from a language perspective means that what is spoken and written is important. Thus, speaking and writing clearly and persuasively matters. This is why public speaking and writing classes are core requirements in nearly all communication curriculums. For Sarah Trenholm (1990), author of *Human Communication Theory*, "The central focus of communication study should be spoken symbolic interaction. To lose sight of this as a primary goal is to lose touch with our rhetorical traditions. Our field began as the study of how people influence each other through the spoken word; a process of continuing interest and importance" (p. 13).

However, many cultures value what is unspoken and unwritten over what is spoken and written. For example, silence is an integral element in Hindu and Jain philosophy. According to Nemi Jain and Anuradha Matukumalli (1994), "the concept of *maunam* is a 'state of becoming' through a deliberate effort of restraining from speech" (pp. 4–5). There is also the concept of *shantam*, which is a "state of being" that connotes peace and bliss. *Shantam* is "an all-enveloping concept covering a wide range of indescribable phenomena such as God, truth, self, being, freedom, nothingness, *maya*, and *nirvana*. The highest truth and bliss are both experienced in *shantam*" (p. 5). Also, nearly all of the world's spiritual teachings tell us that the most profound experiences reside beyond the realm of language and symbols. For example, in the Bible God says, "Be still and know that I am the Lord" (Psalm 46:10). Moreover, many of world's spiritual teachings are all about moving us beyond the realm of language and symbols by emphasizing meditation and contemplation. Finally, many peoples and cultures view the ability to refrain from speaking as a sign of personal dignity, wisdom, interpersonal sensitivity, and mutual respect. In short, in many corners of the world people are admired, respected, and rewarded for using less words and even no words at all.

IV

To view communication in terms of language and symbols is to assume that language makes us social beings. The language that shapes our minds, be that language English, Spanish, Mandarin, or another, is also the same language that shapes the minds of others. Like a community sharing a common well, when we share a language, we also share the worldview of *that* language. In short, no human being is born of a private language, or has a mind that is made of a private language. Language makes our minds public. Further, no language can thrive, much less survive, by being private. Because language is public, language must be shared. This is how language binds us to each other and makes us social beings. This is also how languages survive—by being shared. That we are both using the same language means that we can recognize ourselves in each other. We can understand how each other's mind works. Also, because language can change—and must change to thrive—how we perceive and make sense of things can also change and evolve. In this way, sharing a common language binds us to each other, but never in ways that limit and restrict us. We can do different things, and in different ways, with the same language. Both diversity and commonality reside within language.

V

To view communication from the perspective of language and symbols is to believe that language and symbols create our social and cultural worlds. How we describe and articulate things reflects how we describe and articulate ourselves. Human beings create language, then language creates us. Simply put, language shapes us and our worlds. Presumably, "Language is the principal medium through which social reality is produced and reproduced" (Deetz, 1992, p. 128). Presumably, our social and cultural worlds are different because our languages are different. Thus, preserving our different languages is important in terms of preserving our differences. Also, to view communication from the perspective of language and symbols is to assume an inextricable relationship between language, culture, and mind. Different languages supposedly reflect different ways of framing, interpreting, and experiencing the world. Simply put, different languages reflect different minds, and different minds reflect different worldviews. This is commonly referred to as the Sapir-Whorf hypothesis, named after Edward Sapir and Benjamin Lee Whorf, who formulated the hypothesis many decades ago.

According to Sapir (1961), "Human beings do not live in the objective world alone, let alone in the world of social activity as ordinarily understood, but are very much at the mercy of the particular language which has become the medium of expression for their society. It is quite an illusion to imagine that one adjusts to reality essentially without the use of language, and that language is merely the incidental means of solving specific problems of communication or reflection. The fact of the matter is that the 'real world' is to a large extent unconsciously built up on the language habits of the group. No two languages are ever sufficiently similar to be considered as representing the same social reality. The worlds in which different societies live are distinct worlds, not merely the same world with different labels attached" (p. 69).

For Whorf (1956), "the background linguistic system ... of each language is not merely a reproducing instrument for voicing ideas but rather is itself a shaper of ideas, the program and guide for the individual's mental activity, for his analysis of impressions, for his synthesis of his mental stock in trade. No individual is free to describe nature with absolute impartiality but he is constrained to certain modes of interpretation even while he thinks himself most free.... We are thus introduced to a new principle of relativity, which holds that all observers are not led by the same physical evidence to the same picture of the universe, unless their linguistic backgrounds are similar, or can in some way be calibrated" (pp. 212–14). Evidently, the Sapir-Whorf hypothesis assumes that language is foremost constitutive rather than descriptive. Through language our minds and worldviews are born. Different languages give rise to different minds, and different minds give rise to different worldviews. The point of the Sapir-Whorf hypothesis is that language differences are important, often reflecting fundamentally different things and different ways of processing things. However, this in no way means that communication is impossible between peoples of different languages, different minds, different worldviews. Nor does this mean that our language diversity limits us to a world of moral uncertainty and relativity. It merely means, as Charles Taylor (2016) explains, "that the only road to mutual understanding, and perhaps ultimately agreement on moral and political principles, lies through patient mutual study and equal exchange" (p. 328).

VI

To view communication from the perspective of language and symbols is to believe that language and symbols play a foundational role in shaping our understanding of ourselves, the world, and each other. First, language shapes our relation to ourselves. Case in point, recovery and healing programs often begin with changing the language we use to name and describe ourselves and our struggles. If we name and describe ourselves as a failure, we will experience ourselves as a failure. Language also shapes our relation to others. We can humanize or dehumanize others through language. Martin Buber (2013) made a distinction between I-Thou language and I-It language. Whereas I-Thou language elevates the humanity of the other person, I-It diminishes the humanity of the other person, ultimately reducing the person to a thing rather than a human being. For example, how do you describe and relate to the person coming into your country without proper documentation? Is that person an "illegal" (guilty of violating your country's immigration laws) or a "refugee" (seeking safety and sanctuary as your ancestors once did)? The latter is *I-Thou*, since you recognize your own humanity in the person. In recognizing your own humanity in the person, the person is humanized, deserving of your empathy and compassion. Buber contends that this humanizing of others in turn humanizes us.

Finally, language shapes our relation to society. Language can either cultivate or erode norms of decency and civility in a society—for example, criticisms of government dysfunction resulting from legislators increasingly using derisive and divisive language. The notion that how we use language plays a foundational role in shaping our understanding of ourselves, the world, and each other figures prominently in Buddhism. As the Buddhist monk Thich Nhat Hanh (2013) explains in *The Art of Communicating*, four of the ten Bodhisattva trainings focus on "right speech." A Bodhisattva is "an enlightened being who has dedicated his or her life to alleviating the suffering of all living beings" (p. 52). According to Thich Nhat Hanh, the first part of right speech "is to tell the truth"; the second part "is to refrain from inventing and exaggerating"; the third part is to be "true to your word"; and the fourth and final part is refraining from speech "that's violent, condemning, abusive, humiliating, accusing, or judgmental" (p. 53). In the end, to view communication from the perspective of language and symbols is to appreciate the fact that language represents an important dimension to the human experience. After all, what would be the human experience without poetry, music, literature, and everything else that language makes possible? Even the Bible begins with, "First there was the Word, and the Word was God."

VII

To view communication from the perspective of language and symbols is to believe that power and politics is all about language. Politics in this case is about those things that people struggle over and the means they use to do so. To understand power and politics you have to understand who controls language and how language is used by different people to achieve various goals and objectives. For example, who gets to call whom what, and who gets to use what language and symbols when describing different events, situations, and persons? To view politics in terms of language is to view political success in terms of language. We supposedly win in politics by winning at the level of language. So again, who is linguistically and symbolically controlling how events, persons, and situations are described? Who is controlling where symbols are located? Who is deciding and dictating what language is appropriate, decent, and civil? To view politics from the perspective of language is to assume that words have power. To control language is to have political power. However, if language has power, then what do human beings have? In other words, what are the origins of the power that language supposedly possesses? How exactly does language acquire power? On the other hand, if political success comes from controlling how issues are symbolically and linguistically framed, why do psychologists and political scientists consistently report that our own biases and prejudices shape and influence how language and symbols impact us (see Tappin, van der Leer, & McKay, 2017; Taub & Nyhan, 2017)? In other words, the only language that has power over us is the language we *choose* to have power over us.

VIII

To view communication from the perspective of language and symbols is to believe that language can function either representationally, ideologically, or magically. A **representational view** of language focuses on the ability of language to represent things and events precisely and correctly. This view assumes that meaning resides within human beings. We linguistically represent things precisely and correctly by removing the confusion in ourselves. ("Say what you mean, and mean what you say.") An **ideological view** of language focuses on how language cultivates and propagates various beliefs, fears, values, and ambitions. (Ideology can be defined as those values, beliefs, fears, and norms that make various things appear as natural and normal.) In the words of Frantz Fanon (2008), author of *Black Skin, White Masks*, "To speak a language is to appropriate its world and culture" (p. 21). An ideological view of language assumes that meaning resides within language and symbols. Thus, this view is all about monitoring and contesting what language and symbols are circulating in the public sphere. Finally, a **magical view** of language focuses on the power of language to reveal new truths, new meanings, and new experiences. For example, (1) using writing—as in journaling— to process and understand our frustrations and tribulations; (2) arriving at a new meaning of something upon rereading a poem or relistening to a song;

(3) finding clarity of purpose through chanting; (4) achieving tranquility by praying; (5) calming ourselves by invoking various words and phrases; and (6) changing our outlook by invoking various words and phrases. Viewing language magically assumes that meaning resides within language as a result of us using words and symbols to channel the energy and spirits that are *of* the world.

Simon Ortiz (2003), writing about the nature of Native American languages, claims that "Language is more than just a functional mechanism. It is a spiritual energy that is available to all. It includes all of us and is not exclusively in the power of human beings—we are part of that power as human beings" (p. 111). In many African traditions there is also the belief that language has a creative and generative capacity. This is seen in the concept of the *nommo*—through the spoken word human beings gain the power "to actualize life" and attain "mastery over things." As Janice Hamlet (2011) explains, "In traditional African culture, newborn children are mere things until their fathers give them names and speak them. No medicine, potion, or magic of any sort is considered effective without accompanying words. So strong is the African belief in the power and absolute necessity of Nommo that all craftsmanship must be accompanied by speech. Nommo was not restricted to the spoken word in a public forum, but encompasses all communication situations." Usually, to view language *representationally* is to view language as a tool, and the goal is to use the tool with skill and precision. Usually, to view language *ideologically* is to view language as a device, and the goal is to understand how this device is used to what end and to whose end. Usually, to view language *magically* is to view language as a wand, and the goal is to make the wand do magical and supernatural things. Indeed, to view language magically is to believe that words have power, even a spirit. This is why many cultures outside the Western/European world have elaborate rituals for determining what name to give a child. To invoke a name is to invoke a spirit. As Don Miguel Ruiz (1997), author of *The Four Agreements: A Toltec Wisdom Book*, explains, "Your word is the power that you have to create. Your word is the gift that comes directly from God.... Through the word you express your creative power. It is through the word you manifest everything" (p. 26). Moreover, "The word is not just a sound or a written symbol. The word is a force ... [it] is the most powerful tool you have as a human; it is the tool of magic.... Depending on how it is used, the word can set you free, or it can enslave you even more than you know. All the magic you possess is based on your word. Your word is pure magic, and misuse of your word is black magic" (pp. 26–27).

To view language magically also assumes that language has many unknown dimensions. For instance, *when* a word is invoked, and *how*, and *where*, and by *whom*, can fundamentally alter the meaning of a word or a phrase. Indeed, no poem, no song, no novel, no speech, no lecture ever lends one meaning for all time. One day, for instance, a certain song can mean one thing to us, and another day it can mean something different. It is this mystery that makes language magical.

IX

To view communication from the perspective of language and symbols is to believe that language and symbols have power and can be used like a weapon to destroy our foes or as a tool to make friends and build alliances. Those who learn to use language and symbols effectively will supposedly have the means to attain power. Such persons will often be described as eloquent and charming. Indeed, the most popular book in the history of communication studies is Dale Carnegie's *How to Win Friends and Influence People*. But does language really have power, and, if so, what is the origin of this power? Indeed, if language and symbols are so important and possess so much power, why in the end do people demand "actions" rather than words? In fact, if actions are what really matter, why study communication at all? Can communication function as action? Still, the power of language can be seen in what behavioral economists call framing effects—organizing and positioning words in ways that appeal to our cognitive biases to achieve various outcomes. A framing effect is "when equivalent descriptions of a decision problem lead to systematically different decisions" (Ramos, 2019, p. 224). One cognitive bias would be our tendency to respond favorably to scenarios that are framed positively rather than negatively: "This treatment would save at least 35 per cent of the population" versus "This treatment would have no effect on 65 per cent of the population." We also tend to respond favorably when things are framed in terms of scarcity, such as promotions claiming that a product will only be on sale for a short period and customers will only be allowed to purchase a certain amount of the product.

X

To view communication from a language and symbols perspective is to believe that the ambiguity that pervades language promotes human diversity. The following concepts capture the ambiguity found in language: polysemy (words have many meanings), polyphony (different groups use the same language differently; for example, different races and different social classes using the same language differently), homophony (differently spelled words sounding alike), and heteroglossia (using the same language to accomplish different goals and objectives). The ambiguity found in language means that no language can be perfectly controlled. Words and symbols will never lend just *one* meaning, *one* interpretation, *one* understanding. The ambiguity found in language makes human diversity inevitable and unconquerable. To view communication from the perspective of language and symbols is to either embrace this fact or be hostile to it.

Indeed, according to Mikhail Bakhtin (2008), author of *The Dialogic Imagination*, all languages reflect a tension between centripetal (converging) forces and centrifugal (diverging) forces. Centripetal forces aim to make for a *unitary language*, one that makes for a common worldview and ideological consciousness. The goal is to unify the verbal-ideological world, to make our manner of speaking and writing consistent with dominant values, beliefs, and fears. As such, centripetal forces create and promote norms of speaking and writing that aim to unite people around a common worldview by standardizing and homogenizing our speaking and writing practices. We do so by abiding by the same grammatical rules, adopting the same accents, conforming to the same writing styles, adhering to the same norms of civility, and attaching the same meanings to texts and scriptures. On the other hand, centrifugal forces push language toward diversity by opposing and undermining norms of standardization and centralization. Such forces can be seen in bringing new accents to a language, inventing new words and phrases, violating grammatical rules, employing new writing styles, and incorporating words and phrases from one language into another.

Bakhtin refers to this diverging and converging process as *carnivaliza-tion*. This process is vital for our prosperity by allowing language to evolve and change so as to facilitate new kinds of thought and modes of being. However, many governments and regimes of power believe that fostering and institutionalizing a *unitary language* is vital to binding us to a common ideology that preserves the status quo. As such, such governments and re-gimes of power aim to stop carnivalization, and often forcefully so. This hos-tility to carnivalization can be seen in governments enacting heresy laws, sedition laws, treason laws, and other language laws that aim to limit dissent, diversity, and criticism. Yet in the end carnivalization will always prevail as no language—and no one language—can contain our diversity. As Bakhtin (2008) observes, "A deeply involved participation in alien cultures and lan-guages (one is impossible without the other) inevitably leads to an aware-ness of the disassociation between language and intentions, language and thought, and language expression" (p. 369). This disassociation releases us from "the hegemony of language over the perception and conceptualization of reality." Language now "becomes merely one of many possible ways" to explore truth and meaning.

XI

To view communication from a language and symbols perspective is to be-lieve that language diversity makes for human diversity, and human diver-sity reflects language diversity. Consequently, the loss of language diversity represents the loss of human diversity. Thus, to view communication from the perspective of language and symbols is to be concerned about the fact that at least half of the 6,000 languages now spoken in the world will become extinct by the end of the twenty-first century (Carlson, 2015). Indeed, every few weeks the world loses a language. What will the loss of this diversity mean to us? To view communication from the perspective of language and symbols is to view languages as ecosystems that host and nourish different social and epistemological systems—different ways of knowing, experienc-ing, and understanding the world. With the loss of every language the world loses a cultural ecosystem with many valuable epistemological resources that took hundreds—sometimes thousands—of years to develop.

XII

To view communication from a language and symbols perspective assumes that communication problems arise from our failure to use language and symbols effectively, appropriately, or persuasively. Consequently, the study and teaching of communication should be about how to use language and symbols effectively, appropriately, and persuasively, beginning with speaking and writing clearly and properly. However, what does one make of the criticism that this emphasis on using language properly downplays the important role material, geographical, and technological forces play in shaping, constituting, and influencing communication? Moreover, the problem with the emphasis on speaking and writing properly and correctly is that all grammatical rules are arbitrary and even unnecessary. For example, why must there be subject-verb agreement? Why can't "they/them" be used as a singular pronoun? Why goose and geese, but no moose and meese? Why "you and I" rather than "I and you"? What is inherently wrong with sentences containing double negatives? All of these language rules are purely arbitrary—that is, purely of our own making. All languages inherently possess a set of rules that make our own rules unnecessary. Again, linguists call these rules Universal Grammar. That all languages are born of a Universal Grammar means that all languages are inherently grammatically sound. Also, the distinction between a language and what we disparagingly call a "dialect" is purely political. As Wayne O'Neil, chair of the Department of Linguistics and Philosophy at the Massachusetts Institute of Technology, notes, "Language is not a technical term. It is a political and ideological term" (quoted in Rodriguez, 2003, p. 17). Those who have social, political, and cultural power get to decide what languages we value, promote, and privilege. What is spoken by those with such power is called a language, and what is spoken by those without is called a dialect.

According to Carolyn Temple Adger, senior fellow at the Center for Applied Linguistics, "What makes Standard English standard is a matter of social attitudes and the political power of those who speak the standard dialect.... Because Standard English speakers control education, commerce, government, and other powerful institutions, the standard dialect is firmly associated with public life" (quoted in Rodriguez, 2003, p. 65). In short, linguists view all language systems as equally capable of expressing and accommodating complex thought and condemn our de-rogatory characterizations of various rural and urban language practices. As Steven Pinker (1994), professor of psychology at Harvard University, points out, "Many prescriptive rules of grammar are just plain dumb and should be deleted from the usage handbooks. And most of Standard English is just that, standard, in the same sense that certain units of cur-rency or household voltages are said to be standard. It is just common sense that people should be given every encouragement and opportunity to learn the dialect that has become standard in their society and to em-ploy it in many formal settings. But there is no need to use terms like 'bad grammar,' 'fractured syntax,' and 'incorrect usage' when referring to ru-ral and black dialects ... using terms like 'bad grammar' for 'nonstandard' is both insulting and scientifically inaccurate" (p. 400). Thus, our fear of falling into anarchy and disunity because of our failing to rigidly and institutionally uphold the rules and norms of "proper" grammar has abso-lutely no basis in history or science. It is a delusion.

XIII

To view communication from a language and symbols perspective is to be-lieve that the quality of our mind reflects our facility with language. This is why all standardized tests have a language/vocabulary component. Quantity and quality of words supposedly reflect the capacity of our minds. In other words, to have a command of a vast vocabulary supposedly reflects a supe-rior mind. We therefore commonly assume that scores on standardized tests reliably reflect the quality of a person's mind. However, there is no evidence that affirms any relationship between language and intelligence. How we define intelligence is bound up with our worldview. For example, is destroy-ing our only habitat (the planet) intelligent? Is polluting and contaminating all our oceans, rivers, and streams intelligent? Is manufacturing and prolifer-ating weapons systems that can potentially destroy all life on the planet intel-ligent? Is incarcerating millions of people for nonviolent offenses intelligent? To assume that we can measure intelligence through a language test requires us to first assume that we can measure intelligence and reduce it to numbers. In other words, before we can measure intelligence, we must define it in ways that appear to make it measurable and quantifiable. However, no definition of intelligence is ever culturally or politically neutral. Who gets to define things, such as intelligence, and then coercively and insidiously impose those definitions on the rest of us is about who has the cultural and political power to do so.

XIV

To view communication from the perspective of language and symbols is to reckon with the relationship between language and discourse. That is, is language reflective or constitutive? The popular view is that language is reflective, meaning that human beings use language—like a tool—to perform various tasks and functions, such as creating and sustaining various discourses about different things. Language is supposedly devoid of ideology and politics. It is merely a system of signs and codes. We use language to create discourses. However, another view contends that language is constitutive, meaning that all languages already possess a worldview. In acquiring a language you are acquiring a worldview and being placed in all the discourses that pertain to that worldview. That language is constitutive means that language is full of rules, and these rules become our rules, or the rules that will define us and shape how we engage with the world and each other (see Figure 1.1). Rules govern and fashion our emotional states, mental states, existential states, spiritual states, and physical and material states. As Stephen Littlejohn (1996) points out, "emotions are not just things in themselves. They are defined and handled according to what has been learned in social interaction with other people" (p. 184). We learn these rules in childhood and throughout life, and these rules tell us what behaviors are appropriate. In this way, these rules promote conformity. We have social rules, institutional rules, and cultural rules. All these rules can be found in the shape of our language and how we use language. Our languages uphold these rules. To use language is to abide by these rules, and also to be shaped by these rules. That language is always full of rules means that every language binds us to a language community—others who abide by these rules. Consequently, deliberately transgressing the rules that define any language will often bring negative consequences.

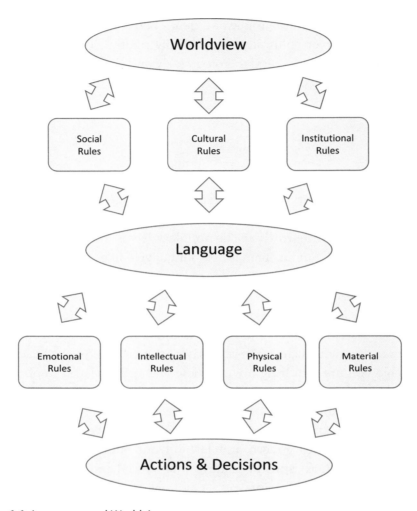

Figure 1.1 Languages and Worldviews

That language is constitutive (laden with rules) means that language fa-vors conformity. It binds us to a community with a common worldview. Consequently, diversity demands violating language, either in terms of using language differently, embodying language differently, or simply adopting a new language that binds us to a different community with a different world-view. There can be no attending to diversity without attending to language. Promoting any kind of diversity demands releasing language of all the rules and constraints—created and imposed by us to serve various ideological and political ends—that limit our ability to embody language in new ways, and by that, our ability to embody ourselves and the world in new ways.

XV

To view communication from a language and symbols perspective is to believe that the study of communication should be about understanding the importance of metaphors. For example, why is war such a popular metaphor in the Western/European world (war on cancer, war on drugs, war on poverty, war on reason, war on Christmas)? Language is inherently metaphorical, which is also to say that language is inherently ideological. As Friedrich Nietzsche explains, "We believe that we know something about the things themselves when we talk about trees, colours, snow and flowers, and yet we possess nothing but metaphors for things which do not correspond in the slightest to the original entities" (quoted in Sousa, 2012, p. 50). Indeed, we are always employing and invoking metaphors to describe persons and events. How "we think metaphorically affects how we talk about problems and the solutions we formulate in response to those problems" (Cunningham-Parmeter, 2012, p. 1548). For Nietzsche, "Metaphors mean treating as *equal* something that one has recognized as *similar* in one point" (quoted in Hinman, 1982, p. 185). To view communication from the perspective of language and symbols is to be concerned with the origins of our metaphors, as well as the implications of our metaphors. For example, how do different metaphors ("a flood of immigrants," "immigrants flowing over our borders") impact immigration policy and discourse? Metaphors remind us that language *constructs* our understandings of the world rather than objectively describes how the world truly is.

XVI

To view communication from the perspective of language and symbols is to believe that *where* language and symbols appear matters, just as much as *who* uses *what* language and symbols. Simply put, the space and place where language and symbols appear is important. Where language and symbols appear reveals much about relations of power and privilege, such as *who* is allowed to say *what*, *when*, and *where*. For example, the anonymity that graffiti affords often creates the space for discussions and subject matter that clash with prevailing norms of decency, civility, and propriety. Yet, on the other hand, marginalized peoples often have no other space and place (such as bathroom stalls) to present topics that are culturally and institutionally disallowed. Graffiti provides the key benefit of anonymity, which protects the writer or artist from retribution. Any person can say whatever, however, and whenever, to whomever they want. In fact, a graffitist acknowledged this benefit in graffiti found in a bathroom stall in response to an inquiry through graffiti about why people engage in graffiti: "It's a chance to vent frustrations, to say things you wouldn't dare speak up about ... because sometimes you feel like letting the whole world know how you're feeling w/out [without] giving yourself away" (Rodriguez & Clair, 1999, pp. 2–3). Indeed, the lack of explicit rules and protocols allows people to express themselves in different ways. Accordingly, graffiti levels the playing field by getting past factors of privilege, such as social status, ethnicity, education, expertise, and experience. It is, in fact, one of the few communication forms that affords such egalitarian virtues.

XVII

To view communication from the perspective of language and symbols is to value how words and symbols sound. The sounds of words and symbols play an important role in communication. For example, the sound of a word, Morten Christiansen claims, can tell us "whether the word is used as a noun or as a verb, and this relationship affects how we process such words" (quoted in Crawford, 2006). Moreover, "adults use the relationship between how words sound and how they are used to guide their comprehension of sentences" (Crawford, 2006). There is also word aversion, which Mark Liberman (2012), a professor of linguistics at the University of Pennsylvania, defines in a language log as "a feeling of intense, irrational distaste for the sound or sight of a particular word or phrase, not because its use is regarded as etymologically or logically or grammatically wrong, nor because it's felt to be overused or redundant or trendy or non-standard, but simply because the word itself somehow feels unpleasant or even disgusting." An example might be the word *retard*.

Then there is what linguists refer to as sound effect words (e.g., *kaboom*). Although these words (also commonly called "animal sounding words") are frowned upon by those who believe our goal should be to speak clearly and properly, Janis B. Nuckolls claims that these words are "elementally expressive" for all languages and make for effective communication. According to Nuckolls, "They add to the existing system of the language by stretching sounds. By doing this, they embellish, adjust, stretch and tweak the language in very systematic and principled ways. So, sound effect words are not randomly thrown together with haphazard sounds" (quoted in Holm, 2013). Finally, noise, as in "Stop making all that noise," is important. Noise means life. When a baby comes into the world, a mother wants to hear crying and screaming. Noise also means dissent and conflict, disagreement and diversity. In short, noise means democracy. A democracy thrives on noise, on people arguing openly, intensely, and passionately, without any fear of sanction and retribution. That noise means democracy also means that noise is a measure of human vitality. It is better to be arguing openly and passionately with each other than silencing each other through rules and norms that limit dissent and conflict. That noise reflects human vitality reminds us that life's vitality, as in the sounds of waves breaking, earthquakes rumbling, volcanoes erupting, forests burning, storms churning, rains falling, and winds whistling, is found in noise. So as regards communication, the sounds and noises that human beings make—and also avoid making—are important. These sounds and noises remind us that human beings experience language and communication at many different levels (cognitively, emotionally, sensually, spiritually, physically, and relationally).

XVIII

Finally, to view communication from the perspective of language and symbols is to believe that our ethics and politics should be about encouraging (even coercing) people to use language and symbols in ways that conform to our own norms and expectations. This is commonly referred to as language politics—the struggle over who has the power to use certain kinds of language, including the power to stop people from using language that may be offensive and derogatory to different groups of people, especially minority groups. The following movements are examples of language politics:

- *National language campaigns*: Initiatives at both the local and federal level to enact laws to make English—in the case of the United States—the country's official and national language, which would demand that all government transactions be conducted in English and all documents be printed only in English.
- *Heresy and blasphemy laws:* Laws that purposely aim to limit the freedom of speech and expression relating to blasphemy, or in any ways judged to be insulting toward holy personages, religious artifacts, customs, or beliefs.
- *Standard language practices:* Institutions discouraging and disallowing slang, dialects, and grammatical practices that can supposedly corrupt the standard and dominant language.
- *Speech codes:* Rules and regulations that aim to stop the infliction of psychological or emotional harm upon any member of a university community through any means of communication.
- *Trigger warnings:* Notices used to warn readers or listeners about any content (spoken or written) that could potentially be upsetting or traumatizing.
- *Microaggression campaigns:* Microaggressions are commonly defined as everyday verbal, nonverbal, and environmental slights, snubs, or insults, whether intentional or unintentional, directed to any person of a historically marginalized group.
- *University language covenants.* Postsecondary institutions requiring—for the sake of promoting civility, collegiality, and diversity—new students to sign contracts agreeing to abide by certain speech codes.

To view communication from the perspective of language and symbols is to view politics in terms of various struggles relating to (1) what language will be the language of politics and privilege; (2) what language and symbols will be used to represent who and what; (3) who determines what language is assumed to be decent, civil, and acceptable; (4) who controls the location of different symbols; and (5) who controls the funding for the preservation of different symbols. However, the criticisms of language politics are many (see the appendix). The most serious criticism concerns how language politics wrongly locates meaning in language. Language politics assumes that meaning resides in words and symbols. In reality, meaning resides within humans. It is us who ultimately determine what words and symbols mean. Thus, whatever power words and symbols possess comes from us. It is us—rather than words—who hurt people.

Conclusion

Language is important because it shapes our minds, our worlds, and the quality of our lives. Who controls what language is legitimate and appropriate is also important. Indeed, language is important because *how* we use language and *what* kind of language we use have many important implications and consequences. We should therefore always use language with care and restraint. However, any power that language has comes from us. We decide what words mean and how words impact us—words have power only when we choose to give words power.

We also need to begin to disabuse ourselves of the many falsehoods found in our common understanding of language. The first falsehood is that quality of language reflects quality of mind. This falsehood can be found in our belief that early language acquisition and the size of a person's vocabulary reflect the quality of a person's mind. However, it is social, cultural, and political systems that define intelligence and also determine what kind of intelligence has purchase. The second falsehood is that (supposedly) superior languages make for (supposedly) superior civilizations. However, linguists and anthropologists have never found a pre-evolved language. The third falsehood is that different languages are superior to other languages (dialects). In fact, all language systems are structurally even and possess the ability to express complex thought.

The fourth falsehood is that languages need human-made rules (grammar) to make communication possible. However, all languages—through Universal Grammar—are already programmed for order. The fifth falsehood is that certain languages are pure and pristine and thus can be corrupted by other languages. In fact, all languages are linguistically promiscuous. Most of the words that form the English language have origins in other languages. The sixth falsehood is that communication demands a common language.

However, does the lack of a common language stop humans and dogs from forming deep relationships with each other? The final falsehood is that sharing a common language is necessary for achieving unity and prosperity. However, did black Americans speaking English stop slavery, Black Codes, and Jim Crow laws? Did Jews speaking German stop the Holocaust? In the end, language becomes a problem only if you *choose* to make it so.

Discussion Questions

I. Would you be comfortable living in a society where there were no limits and constraints on language, and thus you could freely tell your parent, boyfriend/girlfriend, classmates, or neighbors *exactly* what is on your mind?

II. If you believe there should be limits and constraints on language, who should determine what those limits and constraints should be?

III. What do metaphors reveal to you about language and human beings? Can you imagine language without metaphors? Would you want to have a language without metaphors? What metaphor would you choose for communication?

IV. The machine metaphor (e.g., "this team is a well-oiled machine") is hugely popular in the Western/European world. Why do you believe that is? For instance, why must others have to "turn you on" as if you are a machine? That is, why must others have this responsibility to provoke your interest or to make you think? Indeed, when you complain of being bored, you are assuming that others (like your teachers) have the responsibility to "turn you on" as if you are a machine. Also, why must a relationship have to "work" and run "smoothly" like a machine?

V. Finally, why do *only* certain words enter your heart? That is, why do certain words never truly enter your mind? Put differently, how do you know that you are open and willing to hear words (and ideas) that are alien to you?

chapter two

COMMUNICATION AS MESSAGES

|

To view communication from the perspective of messages is to define communication as the ability to convey our messages effectively, efficiently, and strategically. Messages presumably are the foundation of communication. According to Em Griffin, Andrew Ledbetter, and Glenn Sparks (2015), authors of *A First Look at Communication Theory*, "communication is the relational process of creating and interpreting messages that elicit a response" (p. 6). In fact, for Griffin and company, messages form "the core of communication study." In *Principles of Human Communication*, Robert Smith (2001) writes, "communication is the process of sending, receiving, and interpreting messages through which we relate to each other and to our larger world" (p. 10). For William Houseley, Tom Nicholls, and Ron Southwell (2013), authors of *Managing in the Media*, "communication is the production, perception, and grasp of messages bearing man's notions of his philosophy, his politics, and his morality" (p. 90). According to the National Communication Association, which "advances Communication as the discipline that studies all forms, modes, media, and consequences of communication through humanistic, social scientific, and aesthetic inquiry," communication is a transactional process—"a communicator encodes (for example, puts thoughts into words and gestures), then transmits the message via a channel (for example, speaking, email, text message) to the other communicator(s) who then decode the message (for example, take the words and apply meaning to them). The message may encounter noise, which could prevent the message from being received or fully understood as the sender intended" (Parvanta, Nelson, & Harner, 2018, p. 2).

In communication studies, noise refers to anything that interferes in the communication process between a speaker and a listener (see Figure 2.1). Noise is also called *interference*. In *Crisis Communication: Theory and Practice*, Alan Jay Zaremba (2010) views noise as a "factor that reduces the chances of successful communication" (p. 193), and in *The Handbook of Communication and Corporate Reputation*, Craig Carroll (2013) claims that noise adversely impedes communication "without anyone's consent" (p. 305). In *Interpersonal Communication: Everyday Encounters*, Julia Wood (2016) outlines four kinds of noise: "**Physiological noise** is distraction caused by hunger, fatigue, headaches, medication, and other factors that affect how we feel and think. **Physical noise** is interference in our environments, such as noises made by others, overly dim or bright lights, spam and pop-up ads, extreme temperatures, and crowded conditions. **Psychological noise** refers to qualities in us [like our biases] that affect how we communicate and interpret others.... Finally, **semantic noise** exists when words themselves are not mutually understood [using jargon or technical language]" (p. 15).

According to Joseph DeVito (1993), author of *Messages: Building Interpersonal Communication Skills*, "Noise enters all communication systems, no matter how well designed. Noise is anything that distorts or interferes with the reception of messages. It is present in a communication system to the extent that the message received differs from the message sent" (p. 10). According to Maxwell McCombs, professor emeritus of communication at the University of Texas, Austin, the primary question about any message is whether it created "an awareness and understanding" in the recipient. Noise supposedly threatens this process, and thus needs to be removed for communication to be possible. Indeed, from the perspective of communication as messages, noise promotes confusion. We supposedly achieve communication by removing confusion. In *Intercultural Communication: A Reader*, Larry A. Samovar and colleagues (2015) refer to language diversity as a "distraction" and an example of semantic noise. According to Samovar and company, "For effective communication in an intercultural interaction, participants must rely on a common language, which usually means that one or more individuals will not be using their native tongue. Native fluency in a second language is difficult, especially when nonverbal behaviors are considered. People who use another

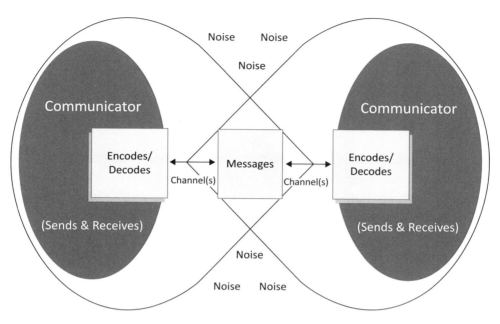

Figure 2.1 Transactional Model of Communication

language will often have an accent or might misuse a word or phrase, which can adversely affect the receiver's understanding of the message" (p. 8).

To view communication from the perspective of messages is to focus on the forces that impede the sending and receiving of messages as the sender intended. These forces often come under the heading of impression (arriving at an understanding of someone or something based on scant information), perception (selecting, organizing, and interpreting a message in ways that conform to our understanding of things), attribution (attaching motives to the actions and decisions of others), confusion (lacking clarity and precision in our description of events and things), deception (distorting, twisting, and manipulating our reality for personal gain), and transubstantiation, which Leroy Wells (1985) defines as "the act of transforming the culture of another group into one's own culture" and, consequently, converting "the symbols and behaviors of others into those consistent with one's own epistemology, or system of knowing and understanding the world" (p. 51). In fact, to view communication from the perspective of messages is to work with the fact that most communication is miscommunication, resulting from problems related to impression, perception, attribution, confusion, deception, and transubstantiation. From the perspective of communication as messages, communication competency is about acquiring the expertise and techniques that allow us to avoid these supposed problems.

II

To view communication from the perspective of messages is to believe that feedback is the most integral component in any communication system. Properly defined, "feedback is the information sent to an entity (an individual or a group) about its prior behavior so that the entity may adjust its current and future behavior to achieve the desired result" (Eades, 2019). Simply put, feedback allows us to correct and control our messages. It makes convergence possible, thereby making communication possible. It supposedly allows us to move from divergence to convergence. Presumably, communication is about achieving convergence, as in moving from chaos to order. For Edward Brewer and Jim Westerman (2017), authors of *Organizational Communication: Today's Professional Life in Context*, "Communication is ... simply necessary for creating order out of chaos" (p. 3). Stephen Littlejohn (1996) claims that **convergence theory** and **information theory** help explain why there is similarity within groups and differences between them, or why groups that share more achieve more convergence, and those that share less have more divergence. Littlejohn (1996) explains: "As communication decreases, the amount of variation within a group increases, the structure of the system comes apart, and entropy prevails. As communication increases within a group, more and more is shared, structure develops, and convergence results. Generally speaking then, the more communication, the greater the convergence, and the less communication, the greater the divergence. People within a group come to share common ideas as they communicate with greater frequency, and they come to lose common ground when they communicate less frequently" (p. 59). In this way, viewing communication from the perspective of messages cultivates a valuing of conformity and homogeneity by promoting the notion that communication needs commonality (such as sharing common experiences, common backgrounds, common ambitions, common struggles, or common training) to succeed. Indeed, viewing communication from the perspective of messages assumes that divergence, as in difference, threatens communication and all that communication apparently makes possible, such as unity, prosperity, and progress. We supposedly achieve communication by removing divergence (noise and difference), and in achieving communication "common ground" occurs. Thus, to view communication in terms of messages is to be about developing theories, strategies, and technologies that will allow us to either limit or avoid divergence (noise and difference).

Ultimately, the notion of communication as messages reflects a racial, ideological, political, cultural, and epistemological hegemon (a dominant order) that views divergence (noise and difference) as a threat to all that is presumably good, such as, to use Littlejohn's words, "common ground." Case in point, Samuel Huntington, chair of the Harvard Academy for International and Area Studies and the Albert J. Weatherhead III University Professor at Harvard University, believes that the United States is disintegrating and collapsing as a result of the increasing diversity from non-European nations. In *Who We Are: The Challenges to America's National Identity*, Huntington (2004) focuses on the supposed threats that multiculturalism, bilingualism, cosmopolitanism, and globalism pose to the prosperity of the United States. He believes that the United States must vanquish these movements to preserve its ideological, cultural, and social stability. It must protect the "American Creed." According to Huntington, the "American Creed," as initially formulated by Thomas Jefferson and elaborated by many others, "is widely viewed" as the defining element of American identity. "The Creed, however, was the product of the distinct Anglo-Protestant culture of the founding settlers of America in the seventeenth and eighteenth centuries" (p. xvi).

Huntington claims that key elements of that culture include "the English language; Christianity; religious commitment; English concepts of the rule of law, responsibility of rulers, the rights of individuals; and the dissenting Protestant values of individualism, the work ethic, and the belief that humans have the ability and duty to try to create a heaven on earth" (pp. xv–xvi). Huntington believes that in the face of 9/11, "Americans should recommit themselves to the Anglo-Protestant culture, traditions, and values that for three and half centuries have been embraced by Americans of all races, ethnicities, and religions and that have been the source of their liberty, unity, power, prosperity, and moral leadership as a force for good in the world" (p. xvii). Huntington claims that Latino immigration poses the greatest threat to the territorial, cultural, and political integrity of the United States. He calls for immediate and severe actions to neutralize all of these supposed threats, which challenge the "existing cultural, political, legal, commercial, and educational systems" and "the historical, cultural, and linguistic identity" of the United States.

Huntington professes to be "deeply concerned about the unity and strength of my country based on liberty, equality, law, and individual rights" (pp. xvi–xvii). However, Huntington's fears have no basis in science or history. The United States has never been racially, religiously, linguistically, politically, or ideologically homogenous. It has always been a creature of both convergence (order and assimilation) and divergence (chaos and immigration). Both forces guide and inspire its evolution. Just as well—communication needs both convergence and divergence to flourish. Even information theory begins on the premise that "the greater the uncertainty, the more the information." Put differently, confusion catalyzes communication. Divergence challenges us to look at things in new ways. It makes change possible by disrupting the order of things. We now refer to this process of disrupting the order of things as divergent thinking—thinking about things in ways that disrupt the order of things that make new and better things possible. Education analysts now promote divergent thinking by advising teachers to give students less direction and instruction. Indeed, most icons were divergent—possessing the courage and fortitude to look at the world in bold new ways and act accordingly. Albert Einstein was divergent. Martin Luther King, Jr., was divergent. In fact, every prophet throughout history was divergent.

III

To view communication from the perspective of messages is to believe that messages can be verbal or nonverbal. Nonverbal messages fall under the headings of kinesics (body language), haptics (touch), proxemics (distance), chronemics (time), oculesics (patterns of fixation), and paralinguistics (voice inflections). Nonverbal messages play an important role in communication. In fact, most communication happens nonverbally, and most people view nonverbal messages as more reliable and credible than verbal messages. On the other hand, viewing communication from the perspective of messages tends to downplay the role that material, geographical, historical, political, and technological forces play in shaping, constituting, and influencing communication. All these forces play a vital role in shaping how we create, propagate, and consume messages. Case in point, the rise of the printing press fundamentally changed how communication was shared and experienced, and by whom. Moreover, messages are always situated in a much larger context, and this much larger context shapes and influences what messages are set in motion. For example, politics and economics impact who controls what messages are put in motion and who gets access to those messages. Finally, no communication is ever outside of and separate from history. That communication always has a historical context means that communication is shaped by the language, ideology, and politics that is of that moment in history. In other words, every political, ideological, and historical moment is either encouraging or discouraging certain kinds of communication.

IV

To view communication from the perspective of messages is to believe that messages (communication) can exceed language. In other words, human beings can use many things to convey messages that have nothing to do with language, such as Native American tribes using basket weaving as communication, Indigenous peoples using rock art as communication, and increasing numbers of global corporations using diagrams and pictures to convey instructions for assembling different kinds of consumer products. That messages can exceed the limits of language also reminds us that human beings have the power to define communication and also determine the purpose of communication. What one group defines as communication can be fundamentally different to what another defines as communication. This is what human diversity looks like in communication. What counts as messages for one group can be different for another group. In a plural and multicultural world, assuming that our messages can always be shared is dangerous. Sometimes certain things must be lost in translation for the sake of communication.

V

To view communication in terms of messages is to believe that intent is important in communication. That is, communication should involve determining what messages people are intentionally sending and receiving. For Gerald

Miller and Mark Steinberg (1975), authors of *Between People: A New Analysis of Interpersonal Communication*, "communication involves an intentional, transactional, symbolic process" (p. 34). The reason being, claim Miller and Steinberg, is that "intent to communicate and intent to influence are synonymous. If there is no intent, there is no message" (p. 35). For Richard West and Lynn Turner (2014), authors of *Introducing Communication Theory: Analysis and Application*, without intent, the study of communication becomes impossible: "If everything can be thought of as communication—our verbal and nonverbal unintended expressions—then studying communication in a systematic manner is not only challenging but nearly impossible.... By defining everything as communication, we inevitably undermine the field we wish to study" (p. 10). That intent is important means that we should be conscious of what messages we are sending and what feedback we are offering. Intent also means that our communication should be judged solely by our intention, and that we should only be responsible for the messages we intended to send. In short, intent assumes that people have the ability to act deliberately. Intent is an important distinction between viewing communication in terms of messages versus viewing communication in terms of language and symbols.

To view communication in terms of language and symbols is to assume that the *impact* of our communication is what is most important. However, to view communication in terms of messages is to assume that the *intent* of our communication is what is most important. This distinction matters in many places. For example, organizations and corporations in the United States are legally bound to have a diversity and inclusion policy prohibiting discrimination and harassment and promoting inclusion and accommodation. These diversity and inclusion policies often begin with a set of guiding principles like, "We respect the rights and dignity of all persons and recognize that discrimination or harassment in any form undermines the fundamental principles of the [organization]. We support a respectful environment through our own actions, encourage respectful behavior in others, and speak out against hatred and bias" (Rodriguez, 2018, p. 1).

These diversity and inclusion policies assume that communication is about language and symbols, thereby also assuming that meaning resides in language and symbols. Consequently, these diversity policies focus on the *impact* of communication—the idea that negative language and symbols make for negative emotions and situations. Sections in these policies read, "the

Complainant has no legal obligation to express discomfort with the behavior or to tell the person to stop or to have filed any kind of ... complaint. The Complainant may have even appeared to go along with behavior such as laughing and joking along with the others. To tolerate something or to consent to something does not mean it is welcome" (p. 3). In fact, "Whether harassment has occurred is determined by the impact on the Complainant and not by the intent of the harasser. 'I was only joking'; 'I did not mean to offend'; 'I thought it was ok'; 'I thought it was all just in good fun' are not legal defenses" (p. 3). However, without the aggrieved person providing feedback to the person who is supposedly doing the offending, and even being released from providing feedback, which again is an important element in a transactional model of communication, how is any person to know someone else is being hurt or offended? Moreover, how could intent constitute no defense? In a world of boundless diversity and plurality, how is anyone to know exactly and perfectly what any one person finds to be offensive and hurtful without wrongly resorting to stereotyping? Still, these diversity and inclusion policies will often end with recommendations like, "Don't do or say anything that could be perceived as harassing. If you are comfortable doing so, intervene when you hear any comments or observe any conduct between others ... that could be perceived as harassing." But what constitutes "harassing" is purely subjective. Appreciating human diversity means recognizing that anything could potentially mean anything for any person. Consequently, intent should matter in communication and to all persons who claim to value human diversity.

VI

To view communication from the perspective of messages is to believe that communication should be about identifying the tactics and techniques that allow us to convey our messages effectively, efficiently, and strategically. In fact, nearly all of the learning outcomes set forth by the National Communication Association for communication majors focus on becoming proficient in the use of messages: "Create messages appropriate to the audience, purpose, and context; Adapt messages to the diverse needs of individuals, groups and contexts; Present messages in multiple communication modalities and contexts; Adjust messages while in the process of communicating; Critically reflect on one's own messages after the communication event; Critically analyze messages; Identify meanings embedded in messages; Articulate characteristics of mediated and non-mediated messages; Recognize the influence of messages; Enact mindful responding to messages" (NCA, 2019). For many communication analysts, the study of communication should be fundamentally about understanding how to avoid and conquer noise (confusion)—anything that interferes with our ability to send and understand messages clearly. Communication problems supposedly arise from our failure to limit and control noise (confusion). Indeed, the most popular theory to arise from this perspective is **uncertainty reduction theory**. The theory asserts that people strive to reduce the uncertainty of others by seeking information about them. This information is used to predict and forecast future behavior. However, to view communication from the perspective of messages promotes a distrust and suspicion of confusion.

From the perspective of a transactional model of communication, confusion emerges as the negation or antithesis of communication. It is commonly defined as a lack of clarity. Also, confusion is seen as something that can be removed or separated from communication. But this mission to remove confusion is impossible, because confusion comes from many different places. First, confusion comes from language. What words and symbols mean is always changing. Also, what words and symbols mean is shaped by context (relational, cultural, racial, historical, temporal, geographical, and ideological). As Gregory Bateson (2000) notes, "without context, there is no communication" (p. 408). Also, confusion comes from human beings. We will never fully or exactly know what any person means or sought to mean, because our experiences are always changing. Moreover, confusion comes from life. As our lives unfold, our meanings tend to change. Further, confusion comes from the world. The world is bound by limits (24 hours in a day, 7 days in a week, 12 months in a year). Our ability to know what others mean is always scant, cursory, and limited as our experiences with others are always scant, cursory, and limited because of temporal constraints. This reality encourages us to make various impressions and perceptions of people that are usually wrong. Further, confusion comes from context. No relational, cultural, political, historical, or racial context is ever clearly and perfectly defined. There is always confusion in terms of defining and determining what is the proper and appropriate context.

According to Corey Anton (2007), "We speak of words as if they help to establish context while we nonetheless speak of them as gaining their meaning from their context; people are said to take words out of context and we often use words to create context. This range of understanding reveals how context (or that to which that word supposedly refers) is anything but clear, distinct, or generally agreed upon" (p. 88). Indeed, according to Jacques Derrida (1977), "a context is never absolutely determinable, or rather ... its determination can never be entirely certain or saturated" (p. 3). A primary reason for this situation is that there are simply too many elements (e.g., race, place, time, culture) that go into determining what any given context actually is. Finally, confusion comes from every medium. Every medium presents constraints, such as space and time (a book can only be so long, a paper can only be so long, an article can only be so long, a movie can be only so long, a song can only be so long, a class can only be so long). Thus, there must always be deletions and omissions, which in turn often make for a certain amount of confusion.

However, if vanquishing confusion from human affairs is impossible, what then does one make of our continuing determination to do so? In other words, what does such a determination psychologically do to us? It undermines and threatens our psychological well-being as a reliable measure of emotional and existential strength and our ability to deal with high levels of ambiguity and confusion. Put differently, to save us from confusion is to save us from the very thing that is vital for our psychological well-being. As Donald Levine (1985) points out in *The Flight from Ambiguity: Essays in Social and Cultural Theory*, a high threshold for ambiguity is necessary "to deal responsibly with issues of great complexity" (p. 17). Also, without confusion there would be no catalyst to look at the world anew. Indeed, under headlines like "The Science of Smart: The Virtues of Confusion," psychologists now report that confusion promotes learning by disrupting our proclivity for familiarity, which tends to come from our deep cognitive structures, which are always searching for patterns and relationships in all things that conform to our worldview. Confusion disrupts these deep structures, allowing us to look at the world in new and exciting ways.

VII

To view communication from the perspective of messages is to recognize that deceit and self-deception figure prominently in communication. We are always distorting, twisting, and manipulating our reality for selfish gain.

Self-deception is evolutionary. Deceiving ourselves supposedly enhances our ability to deceive others, which in turn supposedly enhances our ability to manipulate and take advantage of others for personal gain. In *The Folly of Fools: The Logic of Deceit and Self-Deception in Human Life*, Robert Trivers (2011), professor of anthropology and biological sciences at Rutgers University, contends that self-deception reflects our natural biases and prejudices. First, there is the bias of self-inflation—our tendency to highlight our accomplishments and downplay our failures, as well as our tendency to spotlight our desirable features and attributes and to mask those that are less so. Then there is derogation of others—our tendency to derogate others when we feel threatened. Third, in-group/out-group associations come with different biases and prejudices— in this case our tendency to view favorably those we perceive as belonging to our in-group and to view unfavorably those we perceive as being outside of it. According to Trivers (2011), "Once we define an individual as belonging to an out-group, a series of mental operations are induced that, often quite unconsciously, serve to degrade our image of the person, compared with an in-group member" (p. 19). Fourth, the biases of power refer to the idea that power changes our perception and understanding of things: "When a feeling of power is induced in people," Trivers explains, "they are less likely to take others' viewpoint and more likely to center their thinking on themselves" (p. 20).

Then there is the illusion of control—our tendency to believe that we have greater control in shaping the outcomes of things than we actually do. Sixth, there is the construction of biased social theory—our tendency to develop explanations of things that conform to our own values, beliefs, and fears, which means we subconsciously neglect, exclude, and downplay facts, opinions, and findings that do not conform. Seventh, there are biases and prejudices that come with the construction of false personal narratives—our tendency to unfairly blame others for our own failings and shortcomings. As Trivers explains, "When people are asked to supply autobiographical accounts of being angered (victim) or angering someone else (perpetrator), a series of sharp differences emerges. The perpetrator usually describes angering someone else as meaningful and comprehensible, while victims tend to depict such an event as arbitrary, unnecessary, or incomprehensible. Victims often provide a long-term narrative, especially one emphasizing continuing harm and grievance, while perpetrators describe an arbitrary, isolated event with no lasting implication" (p. 25). Finally, there is confirmation bias—our tendency to focus favorably on facts, opinions, and findings that support our pre-existing views of something and to dismiss those facts, opinions, and findings that do the opposite. In other words, confirmation bias reflects our tendency to respond favorably and positively to *only* those things that support or complement our biases and prejudices. Compelling examples are found in articles with headlines like, "Study Finds that Jurors Often Hear Evidence with Closed Minds."

VIII

To view communication from the perspective of messages is to view communication mechanistically. The goal is to have communication run smoothly and efficiently. This means eliminating friction, stopping our "wires from becoming crossed," and avoiding sending "mixed signals" and messages. It also means stopping communication from "breaking down." Further, the purpose of communication is to accomplish a task—it is a means to an end. Moreover, all that apparently matters is our ability to use communication skillfully, which means being able to calibrate our messages properly so we can achieve our desired outcomes. Also, like machines, communication demands uniformity and conformity to work properly. All the different components—encoder, decoder, medium, feedback system—need to be in harmony with each other. Dissent, conflict, and diversity supposedly stop and obstruct communication from working smoothly. Viewing communication from the perspective of messages assumes that the world is full of conflict between benevolent (positive) forces and malevolent (negative) forces (e.g., life versus death, knowledge versus ignorance, order versus chaos, meaning versus ambiguity, health versus sickness). So just like how machines succeed by conquering chaos, communication succeeds by conquering confusion. Communication supposedly gives us the capacity to rule a world that needs to run smoothly for prosperity to be possible. In allowing us to rule the world, communication becomes integral to our survival and prosperity. In this way, communication supposedly represents our bringing order to the world. From the perspective of communication as messages, communication is order, and the study of communication is *really* the study of order. To view communication in terms of order is to view communication in terms of all that is good. Communication makes good things happen. Confusion, on the other hand, supposedly makes bad things happen. We assume that our survival and prosperity is dependent on us helping the benevolent forces, like communication, vanquish the malevolent forces, like confusion. In cultivating order, communication supposedly promotes stability, commonality, and predictability. It saves us from the ravages of chaos. So the study of communication is supposedly important because communication is vital to our survival and prosperity.

From the perspective of communication as messages, the rise and proliferation of communication machines (cellphones, computers) is a good thing. Such machines supposedly increase our capacity to conquer noise and confusion by giving us the ability to precisely craft our messages and segment our audiences. Our messages can now be revised until all confusion is completely removed. Also, new communication machines allow us to significantly extend the reach of our messages by allowing us to instantaneously send our messages to vast numbers of people. However, are all of these good things really happening? In other words, is the rise and proliferation of new communication machines succeeding in vanquishing noise and making for better communication? Let us also remember that noise—as in confusion and ambiguity—is healthy and necessary. Thus, what does one make of the rise and proliferation of new communication machines that seek to vanquish noise and confusion? What promises to become of us in our determination to end divergence (noise and difference)?

IX

Finally, to view communication from the perspective of messages is to believe that power and politics are about who controls the creation, configuration, and dissemination of messages, and who seeks to resist and disrupt those processes and by what means. In this regard, politics plays out in the contestation of messages. Those with power and privilege need to control what messages are being circulated to allow the status quo to remain in place, and those without power and privilege are obligated to disrupt those messages—as well as the institutions generating those messages—to end the status quo and make for the rise of a new social, political, or epistemological order. Power supposedly resides with whichever side controls the message that is being imposed on us, and ultimately with those who have control of the institutions that control what messages are made available to us.

Conclusion

To view communication from the perspective of messages is to recognize that communication can exceed the limits of language and symbols. There are other ways we can share our thoughts, emotions, and experiences. That we are in no way bound by the limits of language and symbols also means that we are in no way bound by the supposed necessity of a common language. Communication is possible without the need of a common language. All that matters is our ability to successfully convey, either verbally or nonverbally, our messages to others. This recognition constitutes an important contribution to communication studies. Also, different messages have different currency, as well as different implications and consequences. Thus, to view communication from the perspective of messages is to attend carefully to what messages others are constructing from our actions and behaviors. Indeed, people are always reading our actions and behaviors, trying to identify what messages we are sending. As Lee Thayer (2011) explains, "There is no possible way of avoiding being read by others. They are compelled to explain us, with no obligatory regard for our intentions in the matter" (p. 37). However, this kind of reading makes for a lot of miscommunication. This is why, from the perspective of communication as messages, most communication is miscommunication. However, recognizing that such is the case vitalizes rather than diminishes communication. It obligates us to be mindful of all the ways our actions and behaviors can be wrongly construed, and to do our best to limit those things that give rise to miscommunication.

Discussion Questions

I. What does the concept of *confirmation bias* reveal to you about the workings of your own mind and your own illusion of being an open-minded person?

II. Analysts claim that the amount of formal education you are exposed to has no relationship to how open your mind is. How do you feel about that?

III. How do you know when you are learning something important?

IV. Because of technology, human beings are now sending and posting millions of messages each day. Yet, in the face of all this communication activity, human beings are increasingly unhappy, miserable, and isolated. So what is the value of sending and posting all these messages?

V. What do you make of the transactional model's hostility to divergence—the idea that communication demands removing noise and confusion in order to be possible?

chapter three

COMMUNICATION AS MEDIA

I

To view communication from the perspective of media is to assume that the medium is the message, and thus the medium rather than the message (or the contents of our media) is what is *really* important in communication. The medium represents any communication technology—that is, any human invention, such as paper, writing utensils, phones, email systems, texting systems, printing presses, teleconferencing systems, recording devices, computers, tablets, and virtual gaming systems—that human beings use to share and exchange thoughts and emotions. Or, a medium (plural is media) is any human invention that is meant to extend our communication capacity, such as allowing us to transcend the limits of time and space. For Michael Harris (2014), author of *The End of Absence*, the notion of the medium being the message means that "what you use to interact with the world changes the way you see the world" (p. 35). This perspective (communication as media) is commonly referred to as media ecology. An ecology is the relationships and connections between and among things in an environment. Media ecology assumes that in order to understand things, we have to understand the environments that make, situate, and legitimize those things. In this way, to view communication from the perspective of media is to take a systems view of communication, meaning that to understand any communication you have to understand the system that is creating, situating, and legitimizing the communication. Media ecology is the study of how media shape our environments, including everything in our environment, and how our environments shape our media.

According to Lance Strate (2008), professor of communication at Fordham University, the notion of the medium being the message is about liberating "the human mind and spirit from its subjugation to symbol systems, media, and technologies. This can only begin with a call to pay attention to the medium, because it is the medium that has the greatest impact on human affairs, not the specific messages we send or receive. It is the symbolic form that is most significant, not the content. It is the technology that matters most, its nature and structure, and not our intentions. It is the materials that we work with, and the methods we use to work with them, that have the most to do with the final outcome of our labors" (p. 130). The medium is also the message because "content cannot exist without a medium." Indeed, our thoughts and emotions need a medium (speech, writing, drawing, painting) to come into the world. The medium is also the message because the medium precedes the message. In other words, according to Strate (2008), "before we can encode a message, we must first have the code with which to construct it." Finally, the medium is the message because the content of a medium is in many ways simply another medium. For example, "the medium of speech becomes the content of writing, the medium of writing becomes the content of print [books, journals, reports], and the medium of print becomes the content of hypertext" (p. 131).

II

To view communication from the perspective of media is to assume that the medium shapes the doing and experiencing of communication, and that every medium comes with different features and dynamics that impact communication differently. For example, reading an ebook is different from reading a physical book, listening to something on the radio is different from watching something on television, initiating and sustaining a relationship through technology is different from doing so in person, and using a computer to take notes is different from taking notes using pen and paper. Simply put, the medium changes and impacts everything. For example, according to Sian Beilock (2015), author of *How the Mind Knows Its Body*, "the ubiquitous nature of the QWERTY keyboard helps explain a peculiar phenomenon: our everyday vernacular and the particular words we like best in our language seem to be linked to how easy it is to type them. Because we tend to like what is easy to do, we prefer words typed on the QWERTY keyboard with our right hand. It's called the QWERTY effect and has been found in the English, Dutch, and Spanish languages, all of which use a similar QWERTY design" (p. 95). Also, "Names with more letters from the right side of the keyboard have increased dramatically in popularity since the dawn of the home computer and the widespread use of the QWERTY keyboard, and new names coined since the 1990s (think Lileigh) tend to have more letters from the right side than those coined before keyboard use was so ubiquitous" (p. 95).

In a paper titled "The QWERTY Effect: How Typing Shapes the Meanings of Words," Kyle Jasmin and Daniel Casasanto (2012) also report on experiments that found a correlational relationship between emotional valence and QWERTY key position across three languages (English, Spanish, and Dutch): "Words with more right-side letters were rated as more positive in [emotional] valence, on average, than words with more left-side letters: the QWERTY effect" (p. 499). This effect was also strongest in new words coined after QWERTY was created. Moreover, psychologists and neuroscientists report that handwriting versus using a keyboard has significant cognitive benefits. Children learn to read more quickly when they first learn to write by hand and are better able to generate ideas and retain information. According to Stanislas Dehaene, a psychologist at the Collège de France in Paris, "There is a core recognition of the gesture in the written word, a sort of recognition by mental simulation in your brain. And it seems that this circuit is contributing in unique ways we didn't realize" (quoted in Konnikova, 2014). Karin James, a psychologist at Indiana University, also found different levels of cognitive activity when children used pen and paper to do an activity versus using a keyboard (Konnikova, 2014). Other research by psychologists Pam A. Mueller of Princeton University and Daniel Oppenheimer of the University of California, Los Angeles, have found that in both laboratory settings and real-world classrooms, "students learn better when they take notes by hand than when they type on a keyboard." This research suggests "that writing by hand allows the student to process a lecture's contents and reframe it—a process of reflection and manipulation that can lead to better understanding and memory encoding" (quoted in Konnikova, 2014).

III

To view communication from the perspective of media is to struggle with the notion of context collapse. To understand what my words mean involves knowing the context in which my words were either spoken or written, which also means knowing how I am evaluating the situation in which I am speaking or writing. As Michael Wesch (2009), a professor of cultural anthropology at Kansas State University, explains in a scholarly paper on context collapse, "When engaged in social interaction, a person is not only evaluating the situation, but also his own self and how it fits into the situation. Such evaluation is necessary for the person to engage in the conversation effectively ... In short, how we present ourselves (and by extension who we are) depends a great deal on context, where we are, who we are with, and what we are doing, among many other factors" (p. 22). Lack of context makes communication susceptible to distortion. Such is the problem that technology presents. Technology collapses context. With technology, especially social media, you lose the ability to control the context that is necessary for your words and images to be interpreted correctly. There is also no way for us to control and limit the sharing of our original posts by others to audiences that are completely foreign to us. On the other hand, people reading your words or watching your images also lose the ability to know exactly what your words and images mean. You have no way of knowing my intention, and I have no way of knowing your interpretation. Moreover, I lose the ability to adapt and adjust my words to your reaction or observation, and thus the ability to correct your interpretation. In most cases both sides are communicating blindly. Such is the problem that technology presents to communication, yet there is no way to fix this problem. It is intractable. To use technology is always to be susceptible to this problem. In fact, you will eventually encounter this problem. Your words or images will eventually be taken out of context. You will be criticized and chastised, shamed and ridiculed, by persons who know nothing of your intent, motivation, or meaning. Technology collapses context, and, in the process, threatens communication.

IV

To view communication from the perspective of media is to assume that different media proficiency practices (writing, reading, texting, emailing, Skyping, Facebooking, tweeting, Instagramming, blogging, or virtual gaming), besides shaping and influencing the doing and experiencing of communication in different ways, also alter our consciousness in different ways. Case in point, human beings from oral-based civilizations tend to have different kinds of mental and psychological structures than human beings from writing-based civilizations. In *Literacy and Orality*, Walter Ong (1982) notes the following distinctions between the different civilizations: "oral cultures tend to be devoid of cognitive structures that promote geometrical figures, abstract categorization, formal logical reasoning processes, definitions, comprehensive descriptions, and articulated self analysis" (p. 54). Also, "writing fosters abstractions that disengage knowledge from the [environment] where human beings struggle with one another. It separates the knower and known. On the other hand, by keeping knowledge embedded in the life world, orality situates knowledge within a context of struggle" (p. 43). In fact, according to Ong, "primary orality fosters personality structures that in certain ways are more communal and externalized, and less introspective than those common among literates. Oral communication unites people in groups" (p. 67).

   In short, the psychology of peoples from oral-based cultures tends to be fundamentally different from that of peoples from writing-based cultures. Writing-based practices tend to turn us inward rather than outward, which in turn makes for various neuroses and psychoses. Problems with dealing openly, honestly, and transparently with our struggles are common. We also tend to develop a deep fear of conflict and confrontation. Writing-based practices also have a tendency of encouraging us to focus on our interior workings, resulting in our obsession with identifying our intentions and motivations rather than focusing on the implications and consequences of our actions and decisions. Moreover, writing-based practices have a tendency of encouraging us to hold onto the past, thus compromising the power of the present. Indeed, modern technology is now archiving everything, making it increasingly difficult for us to move on from past errors and mistakes. Further, writing-based practices tend to promote uniformity and conformity.

Manuals, curriculums, and handbooks allow us to impose a common set of standards and expectations on vast numbers of people. However, having a vast number of individuals submit to a common set of rules and regulations undercuts flexibility, diversity, and spontaneity. Writing-based practices also tend to promote abstractions and arbitrary categorizations that separate us from reality. In this way, such practices tend to discourage us from dealing with reality on its own terms by pushing us to use language correctly and strategically rather than honestly and courageously. In short, writing-based practices tend to impede situational thinking—the ability to deal with reality on its own terms, as in our willingness to come to terms with all the confusions and contradictions that come with understanding most things.

V

To view communication from the perspective of media is to focus on how the rise of new media is impacting the making and shaping of our minds, and how in turn the rise of new minds is making for the rise of new media (see Figure 3.1). This is captured in the notion common in media ecology circles: "We shape our tools and then our tools shape us." Still, the fact is that writing-based civilizations have always been assumed to be inherently superior to oral-based civilizations. Upon arriving in the new world, Europeans used writing-based practices to measure the worth of Indigenous civilizations. Pedro de Gante (1480–1572), a Franciscan missionary, described the Indigenous population as a "people without writing, without letters, without written characters and without enlightenment" (quoted in Lupher, 2003, p. 244). Bartolomé de las Casas (1484–1566), who is often cast as a defender of Indigenous rights in many history textbooks, said that people who "lack the use and study of letters" are barbarians (quoted in de Looze, 2016, p. 81). Thus, for the arriving Europeans, introducing the natives to writing was seen to be vital to the "civilizing" process. This mentality was also responsible for the forced schooling of Native American children many decades later. Indeed, literacy continues to be seen as the measure of a civilized and cultured mind ("This person is extremely well-read").

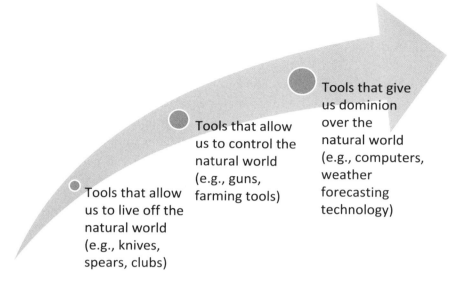

Figure 3.1 The Rise of Tools and Human Evolution

VI

To view communication from the perspective of media is to be suspicious of the claim that the evolution of media represents human evolution. This popular claim assumes that the rise of every new media extends our capacity, thereby furthering our progress and evolution. In *The Story of Writing: Alphabets, Hieroglyphs & Pictograms*, Andrew Robinson (2007) writes, "Writing is among the greatest inventions in human history, perhaps *the* greatest invention, since it made history possible" (p. 7). However, if writing is *"the* greatest invention," why did nearly all the prophets put nothing in writing? The reality is that writing plays an important role in building empires and nation-states (Innis, 2007). Case in point, what does being "undocumented" mean? It means being devoid of the necessary paperwork to show that you belong to a certain place. Paperwork reflects legality, as in having the permission of the government to be of a certain place. For what would be the possibility of empires or even nation-states without paperwork—that is, without the power of governments to subject us to the demands of paperwork (currency, death certificates, birth certificates, passports, social security cards, permits, contracts, deeds, land titles, marriage licenses, visas, etc.)? Writing made possible the first set of legal codes, or collection of laws. These were the Code of Ur-Nammu from Sumer, written around 2100 to 2050 BCE, and the Code of Hammurabi from Babylon, written around 1760 BCE (Khan Academy, 2019). Writing thus extends the power of governments to control us over time and space. So rather than making history possible, as Andrew Robinson claims, writing made a certain *kind* of history possible, one that favors governments. As to why no major prophet put anything in writing, the reasons are probably related: (1) Governments can control who learns to read, (2) governments can ban books, and (3) governments can alter the contents of books by controlling the publishing of books. Thus, in putting nothing in writing, prophets were arguably recognizing the power of governments to control us by controlling the realm of writing.

VII

To view communication from the perspective of media is to recognize that every new social technology is always met with fear and excitement, dread and hope. Plato saw writing as a threat to learning; he believed it undermines the development of our own understanding of things. It makes us lazy. In *Phaedus*, Plato said, "this discovery of yours will create forgetfulness in the learners' souls, because they will not use their memories; they will trust to the external written characters and not remember of themselves. The specific which you have discovered is an aid not to memory, but to reminiscence, and you give your disciples not truth, but only the semblance of truth; they will be hearers of many things and will have learned nothing; they will appear to be omniscient and will generally know nothing; they will be tiresome company, having the show of wisdom without the reality" (quoted in McLuhan, 1962, p. 25). Hundreds of years later, a monk said in a famous tract, *Polemic against Printing*, that the printing press will "corrupt susceptible hearts" (quoted in Pinsky, 2010). What is different now about the criticisms of new kinds of social technology is the highlighting of research findings that consistently show that this new technology is debilitative and destructive. It is said to be delaying adolescence, undermining the formation of deep and meaningful relationships, cultivating mental illness, distorting our sense of self, altering our cognitive structures, and making us susceptible to suicide and self-harm. These findings are found in books by Jean Twenge (2017;

iGen: Why Today's Super-Connected Kids Are Growing Up Less Rebellious, More Tolerant, Less Happy—and Completely Unprepared for Adulthood) and Adam Alter (2017; *Irresistible: The Rise of Addictive Technology and the Business of Keeping Us Hooked*).

Then there are those who view the rise of new kinds of social technology with excitement. This excitement can be found in books by Byron Reese (2013; *Infinite Progress: How the Internet and Technology Will End Ignorance, Disease, Poverty, Hunger, and War*) and Andy Clark (2003; *Natural-Born Cyborgs: Minds, Technologies, and the Future of Human Intelligence*). Supposedly, the rise of new kinds of social technology represents the next stage in human evolution. This new technology will allow us to finally exceed the limits that nature has put on us. It will "supersize" our minds. We are about to become cyborgs, mechanically infused with the best science and technology has to offer. We are apparently on the cusp of the singularity, the final merging of humans with machines. Soon humans will no longer be bound by both nature and culture. Supposedly, there will only be the promise of science and technology. In other words, in releasing us from both nature and culture, the rise of new kinds of social technology will allow us to achieve a liberation that our ancestors could never have imagined. Such is the excitement of proponents of new kinds of social technology, also commonly called futurists.

VIII

To view communication from the perspective of media is to assume that the mind is inherently environmental and technological. The popular view is that the mind is biological. It reflects a set of biological processes that happen within our skulls. Another view contends that the mind is relational. The mind supposedly emerges through our relationships with other human beings. Consequently, the quality of our minds can be found in the quality of our relationships. However, an emergent view coming out of media ecology is that the mind is environmental, meaning that it is bound up with the technologies found in our environments. So as our technologies evolve and change, our minds supposedly evolve and change, too. For Andy Clark (2003), author of *Natural-Born Cyborgs: Minds, Technologies, and the Future of Human Intelligence*, human beings are "natural-born cyborgs" (born of the union between biology and technology). Clark writes, "Many of our tools are not just external props and aids, but they are deep and integral parts of the problem-solving systems we now identify as human intelligence. Such tools are best conceived as proper parts of the computational apparatus that constitutes our minds" (pp. 5–6). In other words, our minds are creatures of our technologies, and our technologies creatures of our minds. "What makes us distinctively human," claims Clark, "is our capacity to continually restructure and re-build our own mental circuitry, courtesy of an empowering web of culture, education, technology, and artifacts. Minds like ours are complex, messy, contested, permeable, and constantly up for grabs" (p. 10). There is supposedly no division or separation between our minds and our technologies. Our minds and technologies co-evolve, and, for Clark, this "makes us such potent problem-solving systems. It is because our brains, more than those of any other animal on the planet, are primed to seek and consummate such intimate relations with nonbiological resources that we end up as bright and as capable of abstract thought as we are. It is because we are natural-born cyborgs, forever ready to merge our mental activities with the operations of pen, paper, and electronics, that we are able to understand the world as we do" (p. 6).

This union of mind and technology is now commonly referred to as the extended mind hypothesis—through our technologies, our minds extend beyond the limits of our physical selves. According to Clark, "We have been designed, by Mother Nature, to exploit deep neural plasticity in order to become one with our best and most reliable tools. Minds like ours were made for mergers. Tools-R-Us, and always have been. New waves of user-sensitive technology will bring this age-old process to a climax" (p. 7).

IX

To view communication from the perspective of media is to recognize that different media have different ideological and epistemological biases. As Edmund Carpenter explains, "Each medium, if its bias is properly exploited, reveals and communicates a unique aspect of reality, or truth. Each offers a different perspective, a way of seeing an otherwise hidden dimension of reality. It is not a question of the reality being true, and other distortions. One allows us to see from here, another from there, a third from still another perspective" (quoted in Chesebro & Bertelsen, 1996, p. 180). Bias also means that different media are seeking to accomplish different things, and these different things matter in terms creating different kinds of social worlds. Computers want us to value information, to believe that the ability to acquire, store, and manipulate information is important. Case in point, taking class notes with pen and paper makes for a different learning experience than taking class notes with a computer. Analysts report that taking class notes with pen and paper promotes empathy, listening, and substantive cognitive processing, whereas taking class notes with a computer impedes learning by separating us from the totality of the learning environment (Dynarski, 2017).

Different media make for different social worlds by promoting different ideological, political, educational, epistemological, and architectural systems. In other words, different media want us to believe and value different things. This is how every media is inherently biased. This is also how media function as a tool of ideology. Harold Innis (2007), author of *Empire and Communications*, discusses the role of time-biased media and space-biased media in making for different kinds of civilizations: "The significance of time and space reflect the significance of media to civilization. Media that emphasize time are those durable in character such as parchment, clay and stone. The heavy materials are suited to the development of architecture and sculpture. Media that emphasize space are apt to be less durable and light in character such as papyrus and paper. The latter are suited to wide areas in administration and trade. The conquest of Egypt by Rome gave access to supplies of papyrus, which became the basis of a large administrative empire. Materials that emphasize time favor decentralization and hierarchical types of institutions, while those that emphasize space favor centralization and systems of government less hierarchical in character" (pp. 26–27). In short, no social technology is ideologically neutral. Different media do the bidding of different ideological systems.

X

To view communication from the perspective of media is to focus on identifying and understanding the social, cultural, and political forces driving and encouraging the rise of new kinds of media, and the social, cultural, and political implications and consequences that come with the rise of new kinds of media. For example, what social, cultural, and political forces made for the rise of cellphones and us increasingly texting rather than speaking face to face? What are the consequences of this change in media? That is, how will this change impact us mentally, psychologically, existentially, and relationally? Indeed, to view communication in terms of media is to be concerned with the trends that are emerging with the rise of social media, as to use a machine is to become a machine ("We shape our tools and then our tools shape us"). We are increasingly experiencing other human beings as machines—that is, as disposable and expendable. We are increasingly entering into arrangements (e.g., hook-ups) rather than relationships. We are increasingly adopting the temperament of machines—expecting things to run smoothly and becoming quickly agitated and frustrated when things and individuals seem to "act up" and disrupt the harmony or order of things.

XI

To view communication from the perspective of media is to grapple with the many concerns and criticisms that surround the rise of new kinds of media, like cellphones, tablets, and computers. One concern is that these new kinds of media are promoting social isolation by releasing us from the hard emotional, intellectual, and existential work that is necessary to form and sustain deep and meaningful relationships. Specifically, new media reduce communicating to connecting, thereby mistaking and cheapening the demands that come with forming deep and valuable relationships. Another concern is that new kinds of media are changing our understanding of what is real, what is important, and what matters. For Neil Postman (1993), author of *Technopoly: The Surrender of Culture to Technology*, this "is another way of saying that embedded in every tool is an ideological bias, a predisposition to construct the world as one thing rather than another, to value one thing over another, to amplify one sense or skill or attitude more loudly than another" (p. 13). Consequently, new media are altering "the structure of our interest: the things we think *about*," changing "the character of our symbols: the things we think *with*," and redefining "the nature of community: [where] our thoughts develop." This changing of our ideology can be seen in our new-found obsession with amassing, accessing, manipulating, and sharing information and acquiring the kinds of media that will allow us to proficiently do all of these things. The rise of new kinds of media is strengthening the notion that communication is fundamentally an informational phenomenon, and that sharing and acquiring information (as in acquiring information about a person) is what is ultimately important. Another concern is that new kinds of media are changing our relation to education. We now view and approach education in terms of equipping students with media that will allow them to access vast resources of information. Now every classroom must be a *smart* classroom—*smart classrooms* will supposedly make for *smart students*, which in turn will ultimately and supposedly make for a *smart society*.

According to Postman (1993), "The computer argues ... that the most serious problems confronting us at both personal and public levels require technical solutions through fast access to information otherwise unavailable. I would argue that this is, on the face of it, nonsense. Our most serious problems are not technical, nor do they arise from inadequate information. If a nuclear catastrophe occurs, it shall not be because of inadequate information. Where people are dying of starvation, it does not occur because of inadequate information. If families break up, children are mistreated, crimes terrorize a city, education is impotent, it does not happen because of inadequate information. Mathematical equations, instantaneous communication, and vast quantities of information have nothing whatever to do with any of these problems. And the computer is useless in addressing them" (p. 119). Indeed, what social problem can be blamed on a lack of information, and thus what technology can solve these kinds of problems? Can any kind of bigotry be blamed on a lack of information? Was the Holocaust born from a lack of information? Was slavery or Jim Crow laws born from a lack of information? Is war born from a lack of information? According to Jaron Lanier (2010), author of *You Are Not a Gadget*, "information is alienated experience" (p. 28). It is "nothing but a shadow of our own minds, and wants nothing on its own" (p. 29). Simply put, information is nothing. Information begins when communication ends. So even though you now have virtual access to boundless information about communication, how much of this information will ultimately be important to you? How much of this information will end up changing how you live, how you relate to others, how you love, or how you perceive and experience things? This is what information as an "alienated experience" is all about. Information has no power or passion to do anything. Nor can any amount of information make us do anything against our will. Which is to say that no amount of *smart* classrooms or *smart* devices can make up for a lack of curiosity and wonder, or an unwillingness to learn and grow, struggle and persevere. Neither can information capture our motivations, intentions, frustrations, and tribulations. As Neil Postman (1979) notes in *Teaching as a Conserving Activity*, "information is not reality. It is an abstraction of it. How high the abstraction or how low, how durable or transient, how precise or gross, how systematic or undifferentiated, how easily repeatable or unique— these will all be settled by the code and its associated material. The printing press, the computer, the television are not therefore simply machines which convey information. They ... conceptualize reality in one way or another. They will classify the world for us, sequence it, frame it, enlarge it, argue a case for what it is like.... [We] do not see the world as it is. We see it as our coding systems are. Such is the power of the form of information" (p. 39).

XII

To view communication from the perspective of media is to recognize the struggles of Indigenous peoples for the recognition and preservation of different kinds of communication media. In *Colonial Mediascapes: Sensory Worlds of the Early Americas*, Germaine Warkentin (2014) notes that "the various objects of knowledge transfer used in the early Americas, despite their physical differences, could be linked conceptually by the fact that in one way or another all of them—codices, wampum, khipu, birchbark, scrolls, petroglyphs, painted skins—served the same social functions that in Europe were served by the book" (p. 50). In fact, according to Warkentin, "Their material differences radically disrupt the narrative that the European codex historically represents, challenging us to revisit our settled concept of what constitutes a book, even to entertain the possibility that the European codex, despite its cultural dominance, is an exception to the norm rather than the norm itself. Perhaps book history needs a new model, one that would accept and develop the book's tendency to metamorphose into various forms, making it possible to penetrate more deeply the complex origins and functions of knowledge transfer using material objects, not only in the Americas, but elsewhere" (pp. 50–51).

For Birgit Brander Rasmussen (2014), "The failure to recognize or refusal to recognize indigenous forms of literacy as writing can be seen as a legacy of colonialism. It is well documented that early colonial agents, who saw indigenous texts as challenges to religious and civic authority, destroyed entire archives of literary culture. In addition, Europeans and their descendants in the Americas developed a possessive investment in writing as a sign of cultural superiority" (p. 144). As Galen Brokaw (2014) explains, because the European world still views writing as an important indicator of progress and civilization, "Even today many scholars seem to feel compelled to pronounce on whether or not the cultures they study possessed a form of writing" (p. 166). However, "One could argue on a number of different grounds that such statements are inaccurate, but disagreements of this kind ultimately come down to how one defines writing" (p. 166). According to Brokaw, "The problem with pronouncements about the absence of writing is not that they are incorrect but rather that the terms and conditions that make them correct are determined by a sociocultural, political, and historical context that is incompatible with the objects and practices developed by other cultures" (p. 166). In fact, "To say that another society did not possess a form of writing has very little descriptive value," as "the perspective that informs such statements sets parameters that make it difficult, if not impossible, to understand the conceptual frameworks of other cultures and how they relate to material practices" (pp. 166–67). For instance, Heidi Bohaker (2014) claims that "It takes only a little familiarity with Great Lakes indigenous cultures to realize the importance of tobacco, and in particular the smoking of tobacco, to regional communicative practices" (p. 124). In fact, "Tobacco smoke is without question a central indigenous medium of communication in the Great Lakes region. The smoke has multiple purposes; it can be used to clear and calm people's minds, to cement agreements, and to convey messages between humans and other-than-human persons" (p. 124). Pipe bowls were also "a medium on which specific messages could be conveyed or narratives referenced." And, "As with other forms of material culture, Great Lakes people could and did use pipes as a substrate on which to inscribe messages" (p. 125).

Elise Wolf (1993) also believes that our common definitions of communication need to be released from a Western/European imagination so as to accommodate and validate the experiences, struggles, and voices of other peoples. Wolf discusses how members of the Tlingit community in Alaska use baskets as communication. The baskets can be read "by noting the changes in the weave and by identifying the many sections of the basket within a particular time-frame" (p. 3). Also, because the "feelings and thoughts of the weaver go into the basket," the "maker and other basket weavers can identify key events and moods" (p. 4). Members of the Tlingit community also use the baskets as "a subversive form of communication," as in using "the making of the basket as an expression of defiance and winning" (p. 4). Indigenous communication practices are also facing extinction in Turkey because of the rise of technology. In this case, the form of communication is whistled. It is called *kus dili*, or bird language, and, according to Malin Fezehai (2019), for "hundreds of years, this whistled form of communication has been critical for the farming community in the region, allowing complex conversations over long distances and facilitating animal herding." However, "because of the increased use of cellphones, which remove the need for a voice to carry over great distances, that number is dwindling. The language is at risk of dying out." Whistling languages are also found in the Canary Islands, Greece, Mexico, and Mozambique. For linguists, whistling languages are altering our understanding of how the brain processes language by revealing that both hemispheres (rather than one) are involved in the processing of language. It was "a long-held belief that language interpretation occurs mostly in the left hemisphere, and melody, rhythm and singing on the right" (Fezehai, 2019). This is no longer held to be true. Thus, what other valuable insights into the human experience will be lost as the world continues to lose other Indigenous languages and communication forms?

In sum, to view communication from the perspective of media is to be concerned with how the rise of new media, especially writing-based media, is increasingly displacing, delegitimizing, and destroying other kinds of media used by Indigenous peoples throughout the world, and ultimately the civilizations of these peoples. If the medium is the message, then what becomes of the world when all the peoples are increasingly creating the same message because of using the same kinds of media?

XIII

Finally, to view communication from the perspective of media is to view politics in terms of what forces are driving the adoption and proliferation of different kinds of media, and who is resisting these forces. Case in point, why should all classrooms now be smart classrooms? How did technology become integral to becoming smart? In fact, how did education become obsessed with technology? Also, how did cellphones become globally ubiquitous, with nearly every human being on the planet now feeling compelled to own one? What promises to be the social and cultural fallout from this kind of global homogenization? How could this homogenization (colonization) be resisted and disrupted? To view communication from the perspective of media is to recognize that no technology is devoid of ideology and politics. There are always ideological and political systems that promote certain kinds of communication media and undermine others, which means that certain kinds of communication media favor certain ideological and political systems and disfavor others. For instance, whose interests are best served by the rise of any communication technology that has the ability to monitor our every move and save all our communication in ways that are searchable?

Conclusion

The perspective of communication as media succeeds by revealing that our communication tools are important. Our communication tools shape the doing and defining of communication. Also, in shaping the doing and defining of communication, our communication tools shape how we experience communication. We become our tools, and our tools become us. Consequently, different communication tools reflect different civilizations, and civilizations change as a result of either the imposition or adoption of new communication tools, or the loss of local and Indigenous communication tools.

From the perspective of communication as media, communication is bound up with tools. We are always using tools, and all tools have different consequences and implications. Also, all communication tools have different origins and ambitions. Different communication tools aim to alter the world in different ways. In this way, communication as media politicizes the study of communication. Different communication tools do the bidding of different ideological, political, and epistemological systems. Thus, understanding the origins of our new communication tools involves understanding the different ideological, political, and epistemological systems giving rise to them. That these new tools aim to finally end noise and confusion is no accident.

Discussion Questions

I. In regards to dating and relationships, would you prefer to live in a world with or without technology and social media? Why? What do you see as the upside or downside?

II. How do you see social media changing the course of human evolution? Do you support these new trends?

III. What would it take for you to abandon any form of personal communication technology? How do you imagine that doing so could actually be good for you?

IV. How would you respond to the following claim: "Connection is not based on how much time we spend with someone or what we do with them, connection is always based on quality of presence."

V. How do you feel about the homogenizing and colonizing impact that emerging technology and media has on the world, especially to Indigenous peoples?

chapter four

COMMUNICATION AS MEANINGS

I

To view communication from the perspective of meanings is to assume that human beings are foremost meaning-making beings. We strive to make sense of things, to give meaning to things. Creating, sharing, and contesting meaning is what human beings do. Life unfolds through meaning, and through meaning life becomes different things to different peoples. In *Man's Search for Meaning*, Viktor Frankl (2006) claims that "Man's search for meaning is the primary motivation in his life" (p. 99). We find meaning by turning outward, by engaging the world and each other. According to Frankl, human beings find meaning in three different ways: "(1) by creating a work or doing a deed; (2) by experiencing something or encountering someone; and (3) by the attitude we take toward unavoidable suffering" (p. 133). The quality of our meanings will depend on how much we can turn outward, thereby becoming completely open to the world and each other. Examples of this outward turning would be honesty and transparency, charity and generosity. Both sets of things heighten life's intensity and richness by pushing us to deal with the world on its own terms and conditions. Frankl contends that through the pursuit of meaning, human beings achieve the means to transform our worlds and our lives. According to Frankl, "man ... determines himself whether he gives in to conditions or stands up to them. In other words, man is ultimately self-determining. Man does not simply exist but always decides what his existence will be, what he will become in the next moment.... Man is capable of changing the world for the better if possible, and of changing himself for the better if necessary" (p. 133).

We decide and determine what will become of us by the meanings we create of things. Moreover, because all human beings have different experiences and must deal with different challenges with different resources, what one thing means to one person can be fundamentally different to what it means to another. On the other hand, there is nothing that limits what anything can mean to any person, which is to say that such limits are purely of our own making. "The important point to remember," writes Lee Thayer (2011) in *Explaining Things: Inventing Ourselves and Our Worlds*, "is that *nothing* we encounter in the world— including words and images—contains or conveys meanings. It is we humans who provide that in every instance. What something means is not what that something means, but what it means to the person making the interpretation of some aspect of the world" (p. 104). Thus for Thayer (2009), "Communication is first of all about interpretations. Nothing comes to us with its meaning inscribed on its back. What something means to you or to me is found in interpretation" (p. 21). However, because all human beings come from different experiences, different backgrounds, different resources, different tribulations, different perspectives, and different places, our interpretations tend to be consistently different. Communication is about sharing, navigating, and challenging our different interpretations of different things. For Deanna Fassett, John Warren, and Keith Nainby (2018), authors of *Communication: A Critical/Cultural Introduction*, "communication is the collaborative construction and negotiation of meaning between self and others as it occurs within cultural contexts" (p. 11).

II

To view communication from the perspective of meanings is to believe that meaning is what *really* matters in communication. According to Vernon Cronen (1998), "Meaning emerges within communication practices" (p. 31). In other words, through communication our meanings of different things are created, navigated, and contested. Also, to view communication from the perspective of meanings is to focus foremost on what is meant rather than merely what is spoken or written. ("Yes, I know what you said, but what exactly do you mean?" "Yes, I know what I said, but that is not what I meant.")

Indeed, when both people are speaking the same language, why are such questions being posed constantly about what exactly does the other person mean? What is making for the slippage between words and meanings, as in what you say being different from what you mean? It means that being communicatively competent is about always attending to four questions: (1) *What is intended*? That is, what meaning is the person seeking to convey? This question assumes that what a person is intending to mean can be different to what the person seems to be meaning. (2) *What is interpreted*? That is, what meaning is being derived from our words and actions? This question assumes that we have no reliable control over how others interpret our words and actions. (3) *What is distorted*? That is, because human beings are of different experiences, different perspectives, different resources, our words and actions are vulnerable to different interpretations and distortions. (4) *What is impacted*? That is, how is the medium in any communication impacting what meaning is intended and what meaning is interpreted? This question assumes that every medium impacts communication differently. These common expressions (e.g., "Yes, I know what you said, but what exactly do you mean?") also remind us that meaning often exceeds language and symbols. Besides denotative meanings, there are also connotative meanings. Many different things shape and influence what things mean to different people. To understand what I mean, you have to pay attention to many different things (see Figure 4.1). In fact, determining what any person means is difficult and complex, as our experiences and worldviews can be fundamentally different. There is simply no way to know precisely or for certain what a person means. As Lee Thayer (2011) explains, "Systems of every size are complex—including conversations. You cannot say something and expect it will be understood as you intended. It lands on the complex minds of other people. They will interpret what you say as they intend—and as is necessary for them" (p. 109). Thus, "In human communication there will always be collateral damage. There will be residual and accompanying effects you may not have intended" (p. 109).

Consequently, communication requires restraint, generosity, and grace. We should give others the benefit of the doubt and be generous in our interpretations of things. We should even be ready to be wrong. As Martha Nussbaum (1997), Ernst Freund Distinguished Service Professor of Law and Ethics at the University of Chicago, writes in *Cultivating Humanity: A Classical*

Figure 4.1 Being Communicatively Competent

Defense of Reform in Liberal Education, "The first step of understanding the point of view of the other is essential to any responsible act of judgment, since we do not know what we are judging until we see the meaning of an action as the person intends it, the meaning of speech as it expresses something of importance in the context of that person's history and social world" (p. 11). For Rabbi Steve Leder (2017), author of *More Beautiful than Before: How Suffering Transforms Us*, injecting "some doubt into our self-righteousness" is necessary for harmony. "Only doubt enables us to consider, *Maybe it's me. Maybe she is right. Maybe he does have a point. Maybe I was unkind. Maybe I was too severe, insecure, self-righteous, proud, or aggressive. Maybe I was wrong*" (p. 116). From the perspective of meaning, communication is "the process by which people interactively create, sustain, and manage meaning" (Dainton & Zelley, 2018, p. 2). Or, "communication is a process of creating a meaning through symbolic interaction" (Adler, Rodman, & du Pré, 2017, p. 5). For William Barnett Pearce (2012), communication arises from coordinating and managing our meanings. "Communication is about meaning ... but not just in a passive sense of perceiving messages. Rather, we live in lives filled with meanings and one of our life challenges is to manage those meanings so that we can make our social worlds coherent and live within them with honor and respect. But this process of managing our meanings is never done in isolation. We are always and necessarily coordinating the way we manage our meanings with other people" (p. 4).

III

To view communication from the perspective of meanings is to assume that meaning resides within human beings rather than in language and symbols. As Virginia P. Richmond and James C. McCroskey (2009) note, "The idea that meanings are in words is perhaps the most common misconception about communication.... No word has any meaning apart from the person using it. No two people share precisely the same meanings for all words. *Meanings are in people, not words*. Therefore, we must realize that what we say to others ... might not convey the meaning we intend" (p. 17). For Sheila Steinberg (2006), author of *Introduction to Communication*, "words are arbitrary signs that members of a culture agree to use to represent the things they sense and experience. It is because meaning does not reside in words that different cultures can also agree that *hond, chien, injha, mpya*, and *dog* can be used to talk about the same animal" (p. 49).

From the perspective of communication as meanings, the study of communication is *really* the study of human beings and the relationships between human beings that make different kinds of meanings possible. What forces, experiences, and relationships shape our meaning of things? Why do certain things (like the Second Amendment to the US Constitution—"A well regulated Militia, being necessary to the security of a free State, the right of the people to keep and bear Arms, shall not be infringed") mean different things to different people? What social and political consequences come from different meanings and the relationships that make for different meanings? As Mikhail Bakhtin notes, "there is no reason for saying that meaning belongs to a word as such. In essence, meaning belongs to a word in its position between speakers; that is, meaning is realized only in the process of active, responsive understanding. Meaning does not reside in the word or in the soul of the speaker or in the soul of the listener. Meaning is the *effect of interaction between speaker and listener produced via the material of a particular sound complex"* (quoted in Volosinov, 1994, p. 53). On the other hand, to claim that human beings impose meanings on things is by no means to deny that human beings use things to preserve meanings. As Mark Johnson (2007) explains, "Meaning requires a functioning brain, in a living body that engages its environments— environments that are social and cultural, as well as physical and biological. Cultural artifacts and practices—for example, language, architecture, music, art, ritual acts, and public institutions—preserve aspects of meaning as objective features of this world. Without these cultural artifacts, our accumulated meaning, understanding, and knowledge would not be preserved over time, and each new generation would have to literally start over from scratch.... However, we must keep in mind that those sociocultural objects, practices, and events are not meaningful in themselves. Rather they become meaningful only insofar as they are enacted in the lives of human beings who *use* the language, *live* by the symbols, *sing* and *appreciate* the music, *participate* in the rituals, and *reenact* the practices and values of institutions" (p. 152).

IV

To view communication from the perspective of meanings is to assume that our meanings are always different because our origins, experiences, resources, and circumstances are always different. Thus, what one thing means to one person can be fundamentally different to what it means to another. For example, what being a Muslim means to one person can be completely different to what it means to another person. As Abdolkarim Soroush, a prominent scholar of Islam, acknowledges, "The essence of religion will always be sacred, but its interpretation by fallible human beings is not sacred—and therefore can be criticized, modified, refined, and redefined. What single person can say what God meant? Any fixed version would effectively smother religion. It would block the rich exploration of the sacred texts. Interpretations are also influenced by the age you live in, by the conditions and mores of the era, and by other branches of that knowledge. So there's no single, inflexible, or absolute interpretation of Islam for all time" (quoted in Wright, 1999, pp. 46–47). Indeed, nothing, even religious scriptures, lends for only one meaning. Yet this in no way means that all interpretations are equally valid. It merely means that there is always the possibility of a different meaning, a different interpretation. In such ways the world is truly boundless.

V

To view communication from the perspective of meanings is to switch the focus of communication away from the sender to the receiver. In popular understandings of communication, the focus is on the sender (or the encoder). This is plainly seen in public speaking (rather than public listening) courses being mandatory in communications programs and departments. The focus is on being fluent and eloquent, making rigorous and compelling arguments, and presenting information that seduces and appeals to different audiences. We assume that the sender plays the primary role in any communication situation. It is the sender who apparently has the ability and the means to make various things possible. Using language and symbols, the sender conveys, the sender persuades, the sender propagates, the sender shapes, the sender calibrates, the sender imposes, and the sender manipulates. However, from the perspective of meanings, the receiver is who is really important. It is the receiver who will ultimately decide what things mean. As Lee Thayer (2009) explains, "A person may be listening to you. But what that person is hearing is not what you said, but her own interpretation of what you may (or may not) have said. All the actual consequences of any communication encounter flow from the interpretations that people make of things. That may or may not be what you intended. But the power player in any communication situation is the *receiver*, not the *sender*" (p. 34). As such, "All consequences flow from how the receiver interprets things" (p. 34).

To view communication from the perspective of meanings is to view power as residing within the realm of interpretation rather than the realm of transmission or persuasion. That I have the ability to shape what things mean means that I have the ability to control how I respond to things and persons, and how I allow either to impact me. It also means that I am responsible for how I choose to respond to things as all interpretations have implications and consequences. So regardless of what the sender intends, what the receiver interprets matters.

VI

To view communication from the perspective of meanings is to value the tension between intention and interpretation (see Figure 4.2). Our words, actions, and decisions will always be open to different interpretations. We will never be able to completely or perfectly control how others choose to interpret our words, actions, and decisions. On the other hand, others will never be capable of reliably knowing our intentions and motivations, or the reasons behind our words, actions, and decisions. Consequently, both sides (the side of interpretation, and the side of intention) will always make mistakes and misjudgments. Yet these mistakes and misjudgments form the natural rhythm of communication, just like how waves form the natural rhythm of oceans. Communication will never be perfect. We will always be making mistakes and misjudgments. In this way, the flourishing of communication demands grace, patience, and forbearance. We will never be able to perfectly control the realm of interpretation, nor the realm of intention. Yet embracing these limitations enriches communication by pushing us to recognize that our words, actions, and decisions, regardless of our most strenuous efforts, will always be susceptible to all manner of interpretations. Consequently, caution is necessary. We must always be sensitive to the possibility of an interpretation that is beyond our imagination, which again reminds us of why grace, patience, and forbearance are necessary for the flourishing of communication. On the other hand, the best any person could offer of our words, actions, and decisions are interpretations. Our interpretations are nothing but our own creations, reflecting our biases, beliefs, values, fears, and suspicions. Simply put, interpretations are human things. We promote and vitalize communication by recognizing the limits of our interpretations and always examining the forces and experiences that are shaping and influencing our own meanings of things.

VII

To view communication from the perspective of meanings is to define the study of communication as how human beings create, navigate, coordinate, manage, and challenge meanings. This is supposedly the hallmark of the

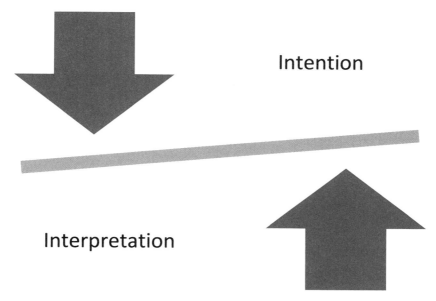

Figure 4.2 The Core Tension in Communication

human experience: us creating, navigating, and challenging meanings. To view the study of communication from the perspective of meanings is to believe that the study of communication should focus on how social and institutional forces impact the creation and propagation of different meanings. In other words, to view communication in terms of meaning is to believe that the study of communication should focus on all the forces, structures, and institutions that affect how human beings make, share, and propagate meanings. In this regard, the study of communication should presumably draw from sociology, psychology, biology, and anthropology. How do we arrive at our meanings of things and persons? What forces encourage or discourage the rise of various meanings?

VIII

To view communication from the perspective of meanings is to believe that meaning is always in flux, always moving, shifting, and changing. What I mean this morning can be different from what I mean this evening. Indeed, our meanings are always shifting and changing because of all kinds of forces. When our experiences change, our meanings tend to change. When our contexts change, our meanings tend to change. When our resources change, our meanings tend to change. When our circumstances change, our meanings tend to change. When our environments change, our meanings tend to change. As David Bohm (1985) explains in *Unfolding Meaning*, "There is an inherent ambiguity in any concrete meaning. That is to say, how meanings arise and what they signify depends to a large extent on what a given situation means to us, and this may vary according to our interests and motivations, our backgrounds of knowledge, and so on" (p. 83). Simply put, as we change, our meanings change. That meaning is always in flux means that assumptions are a problem in communication. From the perspective of meaning, communication involves cultivating a mind that is vigilant about our assumptions so that communication is never compromised by assumptions. Such a mind is always probing, contesting, and challenging the assumptions that others and ourselves make. Indeed, failing to notice our assumptions makes us intellectually and emotionally lazy, undermining our ability to be open to new meanings of things and persons.

IX

To view communication from the perspective of meanings is to believe that communication arises from the achievement of a *shared* meaning—a meaning that works for both of us. For example, you will never know exactly or perfectly what I mean when I say "I love you," and I will never exactly and perfectly know what you mean when you say that you love me. Communication is about us coming to a *shared* meaning of what each of us means. It is about approximation. Even though I will never know for certain what you mean, and you will never know for certain what I mean, all that matters is that we have a good sense of what each other means. That communication is about approximation means that communication will never be complete and absolute. We will always be guessing, triangulating, and approximating. This again is why being generous in our descriptions and interpretations of things and people is important to achieving communication. In most cases, communication problems arise from a lack of generosity rather than from our failure to correctly guess each other's meanings. On the other hand, to view communication from the perspective of meanings is to believe that our communication problems arise from our failure to create a shared meaning. This can supposedly happen because our perspectives are different, our experiences are different, our assumptions are different, our expectations are different, or our intentions are different. It can also happen because of our unwillingness to try hard enough to understand what the other person means or is trying to mean. In other words, from the perspective of communication as meanings, our communication problems have nothing much to do with language and symbols. Many factors can obstruct our coming to a shared meaning, such as our unwillingness to listen—truly listen—to things that are difficult and probably unfair. As Alphonso Lingis (1994) notes, "To enter into conversation with another is to lay down one's arms and one's defenses; to throw open the gates of one's own positions; to expose oneself to the other, the outsider; and to lay oneself open to surprises, contestation, and inculpation" (p. 87). To view communication from the perspective of meaning is to recognize that communication is often difficult and demanding. It involves an enormous amount of work and effort as achieving a shared meaning can be difficult.

X

To view communication from the perspective of meanings is to believe that meaning and context are bound up with each other. Meanings shape contexts, and contexts shape meanings. To know our meanings of things involves knowing the context that is situating and locating our meanings. Communication problems supposedly arise from our failure to properly understand the context that is locating our meanings. But determining any context is difficult. To begin with, there are different kinds of contexts. There can be a racial context, a relational context, a cultural context, a historical context, and even a personal context. There is no way to know exactly what context is in play. Also, what I conceive and perceive to be the proper context can be different from what you conceive and perceive to be the proper context. Contexts also mean that what I find to be appropriate can be different from what you find to be appropriate. Finally, contexts are fleeting and always changing. Because contexts are always changing, meanings are always changing. In this regard, context presents many challenges to communication with regard to knowing what a person means. This is why restraint is important in communication. We should emphasize probing and exploring rather assuming and concluding: "What exactly did you mean by that?" rather than, "How could you say something so offensive?"

In many ways the problem of communication is the problem of context. We attend to communication by attending to context. Finally, because context shapes meaning, whoever decides what is the proper or correct context possesses power. That is, power resides with the person who decides what is the right place and time to say certain things. However, such power is always arbitrary, as the determination of context is shaped purely by human beings and has nothing to do with the workings of the natural world. In the end, understanding the nature of context is about recognizing and remembering the following: First, *context is multifaceted*. That is, context has many different dimensions (racial, cultural, political, historical, social, temporal, geographical), which means that any word or symbol, in being bound by context, can always lend itself for all kinds of different and conflicting meanings. Second, *context is indeterminate*. That is, there is simply no way for different people to know what context is in play or governing the situation. What things mean to one person could mean something different to another. Finally, *context is political*. That is, context is always serving an ideological master. Who determines what is the appropriate time and space to say anything has power. Yet upon what legitimate basis is such power achieved?

XI

To view communication from the perspective of meanings is to believe that any meaning-making process is also an identity-making process and a reality-making process. In creating meanings we create ourselves and our social worlds. Consequently, our conceptions and perceptions of ourselves and our worlds are bound up with how we conceive and experience communication. Problems that pertain to our conceptions of ourselves are fundamentally communication problems. Indeed, a popular misconception is that our identity is stable and bound by boxes ("I am a white, heterosexual, Jewish, woman"). However, what being white means to one person can be fundamentally different for others, just like what being heterosexual, Jewish, or a woman means to one person can be different for others. In short, there is no one definition of any identity marker. Through communication we form our conceptions of ourselves, which is to say that through communication we recognize what things *mean* to us and which people matter to us. This is the stuff of identity—our recognizing the things and people that matter to us. However, due to time and space, these things and people will eventually change.

So the woman who is a mother today was a daughter many years ago, and the person who is now the president of an international bank was an environmental activist in school. Times change, people change; circumstances change, people change; environments change, people change. So as our lives change because of the changing nature of time and space, how we perceive, describe, and experience ourselves also change. Social problems are also fundamentally communication problems, which means that fixing any social problem involves changing the communication that surrounds that problem. Indeed, no social problem falls from the sky. Certain things must be defined, constituted, and languaged as social problems. There must also be agreement on what constitutes a social problem, and such agreement is achieved through communication. In short, all of these processes happen in communication and belong to a certain kind of communication ecology. No social problem is ever outside or separate from a certain kind of communication ecology. What one society can view as a social problem can *mean nothing* in another society.

XII

To view communication from the perspective of meanings is to recognize that our meanings are always being contested and challenged. There will never be consensus on what things mean as, again, our origins, experiences, and circumstances will always be different. For example, what does being civil mean? What does being offensive mean? What does being a good teacher mean? What does being a good student mean? What does being a feminist mean? What does being a Christian mean? What does being a Muslim mean? Instead, what is always at work are attempts and initiatives to create the impression that various things only convey, and *can* only convey, one meaning.

Enter the notion of the ideograph. It is tool of ideology, used to sustain and protect the hegemony of a certain kind of ideology. Hegemony refers to a dominant set of conceptual and material arrangements that shape how we perceive, experience, and make sense of things. An ideograph is an abstraction, born purely from a system of beliefs, fears, and values that seek to foster a certain way of viewing and experiencing the world. Ideographs "function as guides, warrants, reasons, or excuses for behavior" (McGee, 1980, p. 6). The purpose of an ideograph is to have us all share a common set of meanings, and thus a common ideology (a common system of beliefs, values, fears, ambitions, and norms) that reinforces a certain hegemony or hegemon. Ideographs are ideological Trojan horses. Examples of ideographs include normal, civility, family values, patriot, liberty, privacy, freedom, democracy. Note how these ideographs simply pass as conventional wisdom. That is, being normal, or civil, or a patriot is simply assumed to be a good thing; valuing democracy or supporting family values is simply assumed to be a good thing. But where did all these notions come from? Why should being normal matter, and who decides what being normal or civil means? Again, nothing lends itself to one meaning and will never lend itself to *just* one meaning. Human diversity is also about diversity of experiences, diversity of circumstances, diversity of perspectives, and diversity of meanings. In sum, viewing communication in terms of meanings promotes a pluralistic and democratic sensibility. There is always a recognition and appreciation that there are different meanings of things and persons. Nothing lends itself to only one meaning.

XIII

To view communication from the perspective of meanings is to appreciate the difference between descriptive language and evaluative language. Most communication problems have origins in us mistaking evaluative language for descriptive language. Evaluative language reflects and privileges our own values, beliefs, fears, and prejudices. Claiming that a person speaks loudly, or is lazy, or is rude, or is offensive is evaluative rather than descriptive. Possibly, the person you are describing as rude was merely seeking to be honest; or the person you are describing as lazy could merely be tired or bored; or the person you are describing as loud is merely seeking to be heard and acknowledged. Evaluative language tends to promote hostility and resentment, since the person you are judging and characterizing is no doubt convinced that you have no right to do so. Indeed, the problem with evaluative language is that it reveals no recognition of the fact that our interpretations reflect our own subjectivity. Evaluative language is about us imposing our subjectivity on others. For again, why should the person who is merely seeking to be honest be judged and characterized by us as being rude and offensive? How did we come to have such a right to make such a negative characterization? This is also how evaluative language undermines communication—our interpretations (meanings) of something become an evaluation of someone and something. Ideally, our focus should be on observing and describing rather than evaluating and condemning.

XIV

Finally, to view communication from the perspective of meanings is to believe that power and politics is about who determines the meaning of things. That is, from the perspective of communication as meaning, politics is about who controls the meaning of things, and who is seeking to disrupt those meanings. So who determines what being offensive means? Who determines what marriage means? Who determines what being a Christian means? Who determines what terrorism means? Who determines what liberty means? Who determines what being civil means? Who determines what equality means? Who determines what justice means? Case in point, the Declaration of Independence states, "We hold these truths to be self-evident, that all men are created equal, that they are endowed by their Creator with certain unalienable Rights, that among these are Life, Liberty and the pursuit of Happiness—That to secure these rights, Governments are instituted among Men, deriving their just powers from the consent of the governed—That whenever any Form of Government becomes destructive of these ends, it is the Right of the People to alter or to abolish it, and to institute new Government, laying its foundation on such principles and organizing its powers in such form, as to them shall seem most likely to effect their Safety and Happiness." But what do these words mean when slavery was and continued to be the law of the land when this declaration was made in the US Congress? No doubt, what these words meant for slaves was fundamentally different than what they meant to those who created and legalized this document. In fact, the words in the declaration still mean different things to different peoples. The struggle over what words and symbols mean can also be seen in how the US Constitution is legally and philosophically engaged.

A popular legal philosophy that many judges, legal scholars, and Supreme Court justices employ in understanding the Constitution is called originalism. Originalism is a principle of interpretation that contends that the Constitution "should be interpreted in accordance with its original meaning—that is, the meaning it had at the time of its enactment" (Blake, 2017). In other words, understanding the Constitution's meaning requires us to go back to 1776 and identify either what was meant by those who drafted and ratified the Constitution, or what "reasonable persons" living at the time of its adoption would have understood the "ordinary meaning" of the Constitution to be. Originalism demands that those of us who live in the twenty-first century be morally and legislatively ruled by those who lived in the seventeenth century. According to Robert Bork (2005), "Originalism means that the judge should interpret the Constitution according to the principles originally understood by the men who ratified it and made it law" (p. xxx). However, how does one know over 200 years later precisely what all those people meant in 1776, especially when all human beings have different experiences, resources, circumstances, and ambitions, ultimately making for different interpretive schemes? In fact, why should the descendants of all the peoples who were enslaved, marginalized, and disenfranchised in 1776 now be morally and legislatively obligated to find and uphold the meanings of those who held their ancestors in servitude and bondage? Indeed, which group benefits most from preserving the meanings of the people who ruled the United States in 1776?

According to Ken Levy (2017), "Originalism says that if the words are at all unclear, then judges need to consult historical sources to determine their meaning at the time of ratification, and the correct application of these words to new cases should clearly follow." However, as Levy explains in a column in the *New York Times*, this is exactly the problem, as the meanings of many words and phrases in the Constitution are ambiguous, such as "right," "unreasonable," "probable cause," "due process," "excessive," "cruel and unusual," and "equal protection." According to Levy, "even if we could find clear definitions of these terms in a dictionary, current or historical, applying these definitions to cases that the founders did not anticipate only expands the range of ambiguity (and therefore interpretive possibilities)." Levy claims that the founders deliberately used ambiguous language so to invite future generations "to interpret and reinterpret" the words in the Constitution to allow the Constitution to adapt to new values, circumstances, and challenges. In other words, the founders purposely used ambiguity to make the Constitution a living document, one that can bend and adapt, evolve and change. This seems a plausible position, as the founders left no instructions or directions on how to approach or interpret the Constitution. Also, the Constitution says nothing about many important issues. As Jill Lepore (2017a), professor of American history at Harvard University, observes, "The Constitution and the Bill of Rights say nothing about sex, of any kind, with anyone, under any circumstances. Nor do any of the original state constitutions." Moreover, as much as human beings create and propagate meanings, human beings also undermine and discourage "Other" meanings to protect the status quo by blocking open conflict and dissent. Both processes happen in communication.

In *Democracy in an Age of Corporate Colonization: Developments in Communication and the Politics of Everyday Life*, Stanley Deetz (1992) discusses the different ways that "Other" meanings are suppressed and discouraged for the sake of avoiding conflict and dissent:

- One of the most common is the disqualification of certain groups or participants. Disqualification can "occur through the denial of the right of expression, denying access to speaking forums, the assertion of the need for certain expertise in order to speak" (p. 187). For example, "You are white, what do you know about racism?"
- Then there is naturalization—"one view of the subject matter is frozen as the way the thing is. In this process, the constitution process is closed to inspection and discussion" (p. 190). In other words, naturalization means treating something that is produced by human beings as natural and belonging to the world. For example, "How could you possibly say something so offensive?" In this case, what is judged to be offensive is assumed to be made by nature rather than human beings.
- Then there is neutralization—"the values in the construction process are forgotten as arbitrary" (p. 191). There are always human values in communication. To make believe that any communication is devoid of values

is neutralization. For example, "That is such a vulgar thing to say. You should be ashamed of yourself." However, one person's vulgarity can be another person's honesty.

- Then there is topic avoidance—"every social group prohibits or discourages the discussion of some events and feelings." For example, "This conversation is making me really uncomfortable. Let's discuss something else."

- There is also subjectification of experience—invoking one's opinion to stop any further discussion. For example, "This is simply how I feel, and I would appreciate if you would respect that and let us move on."

- Then there is plausible deniability—using ambiguity to conceal one's true position or opinion. For example, "I never said your presentation was horrible. I only said it needs a lot of work. No need to get hostile."

- There is also legitimation—rationalizing and justifying decisions and practices by invoking higher order explanatory devices. That is, using larger moral and ideological frameworks to justify various decisions and courses of action. For example, "Because I am a Christian, I simply cannot support your position on that matter." However, there is no one definition of anything, including what being a Christian means. Legitimation is about masking that fact.

- Finally, there is pacification—"the process by which conflictual discussion is diverted or subverted through an apparently reasonable attempt to engage in it" (p. 196). According to Deetz, "Messages that pacify tend to discount the significance of the issue, the solvability of the issue, or the ability of the participant to do anything about the issue" (pp. 196–97). For example, "Yes, I know this is an important issue and it matters a great deal to you. I get that, and I really want to help you. But I doubt Congress is ready to take on such a divisive issue." But why must the matter be framed divisively, and who is assuming that the matter is inherently divisive?

Conclusion

That a Jackson Pollock painting can be valued at over $100 million makes plain that meaning ultimately resides within human beings. It also reminds us that our meaning of things is bound up with our values, beliefs, fears, resources, and experiences. Consequently, identifying or understanding another person's meaning of something can often be challenging, as our values, beliefs, fears, resources, and experiences tend to be different. From the perspective of communication as meanings, communication becomes archeology. We should be always patiently and carefully probing a person to understand what that person means. Nothing should ever be assumed. From the perspective of communication as meanings, human diversity is boundless. In being of different values, beliefs, fears, resources, and experiences, every human being is different. Again, who can fathom that a Jackson Pollock painting can be worth so much money, or that any person would be willing to pay so much for a painting? From the perspective of communication as meanings, communication is about understanding rather than informing or persuading. Our goal is to understand the other person's meaning of things, rather than trying to coercively impose our meaning of things on the person. In this way, our focus is always on the other. What can I do to understand your meaning of things?

Discussion Questions

I. What does the notion that meanings are inherently unstable and unreliable mean to you?

II. Who should have the power to determine the meaning of your words and actions? Why? What does your position mean for your politics? That is, what do you see as the implications of your position?

III. Do you agree with the thesis that civility can be a threat to communication? That is, why should my meaning of something conform to your sensibility or else face scorn and sanction?

IV. If meaning is ultimately found in human beings, rather than in language, how does that now impact your ethics and politics?

V. How do you see racial, social, cultural, and political forces disrupting and contesting our meaning of things? When and how much of these processes are vital?

chapter five

COMMUNICATION AS NARRATIVES

To view communication from the perspective of narratives is to assume that we are narrative beings. We are *"homo narrans."* We are storytellers. We make sense of the world, ourselves, and each other by the stories we create, share, and consume. For Alasdair MacIntyre (2007), "man is in his actions and practice, as well as in his fictions, essentially a story-telling animal" (p. 216). To view human beings as storytellers is to challenge the claim that human beings are information-seeking, information-processing, and information-consuming beings. Indeed, the reality of *confirmation bias* calls into question our ability to respond to information rationally and objectively. Moreover, to view communication from the perspective of narratives is to believe that narratives play an important role in shaping and cultivating our humanity. In an essay, "The Power of Stories," Scott Russell Sanders (1997) discusses the many aspects of this important role: "Stories entertain us; create community; help us see through the eyes of other people; show us the consequences of our actions; educate our desires; help us to dwell in place; help us to dwell in time; help us to deal with suffering, loss, and death; teach us how to be human; and acknowledge the wonder and mystery of Creation" (p. 115). For David Engen (2002), stories also help us participate in a community, take responsibility for our actions, explore "new dimensions of social suffering," "savor certain dimensions of [the] world," and ultimately help us "become more fully human" (p. 55). In the words of Martin Cortazzi (2001), "through life stories individuals and groups make sense of themselves; they tell what they are or what they wish to be, as they tell so they become, they are their stories" (p. 388). Hans Ladegaard (2017) claims that narratives perform a deep psychological function: "people use them to make sense of themselves and their world" (p. 31). This kind of narration, according to Ladegaard, makes for identities that are always "embedded in a particular cultural and historical context." In other words, the narrative process "creates identities which are continuously remade, highly situational, sometimes even contradictory" (p. 31). To have an identity is to have a story. However, because no person is ever of one story (as no person is ever of one cultural and historical context), no person is ever of one identity. As our experiences change, our stories change, and as our stories change, our identities change.

II

To view communication from the perspective of narratives is to believe communication is a narrative-making, narrative-negotiating, narrative-contesting, and narrative-sharing practice. A narrative is about putting things together in ways that reflect and affirm our own values, beliefs, fears, and biases. We never simply present the truth or the facts. We select, adjust, omit, and even invent things and events in ways that are coherent to us, or in ways that *appear* to make things coherent for us. That communication is a narrative practice means that communication fundamentally involves processes of selection, omission, distortion, elaboration, and even invention. There is always fiction in communication. No person is ever telling the complete and absolute truth. Words, claims Thayer (1983), "have no claim upon truth [and] neither do facts.... A fact is a fact only because it is interpretable in some way" (p. 137). Thus, Oscar Wilde advises that "We should live our life as a form of fiction. To be a fact is to be a failure" (quoted in Chamberlin, 2003, p. 124).

III

To view communication from the perspective of narratives is to measure communication competency by efficacy and proficiency—being a proficient and commanding storyteller. That is, what really matters is who is telling the story, what the story is about, how the story is being told, and what means or devices are being used to tell the story. Again, the quality of the facts is secondary. What matters is the ability to present a story convincingly, or in ways that appeal to the emotions and passions of those listening to the story. A narrative perspective believes that appealing to our emotions and passions is the pathway to persuasion, since the mind is bound up with the body. Indeed, under headlines like "The Backfire Effect: Why Facts Don't Win Arguments," analysts point to how human beings are susceptible to emotions and passions. Even when misinformed people, particularly political partisans, are "exposed to corrected facts in news stories, they rarely [change] their minds. In fact, they often [become] even more strongly set in their beliefs" (Keohane, 2010). In short, facts seem to have no ability to cure misinformation. In fact, "facts could actually make misinformation even stronger" (Keohane, 2010). Discussing why this is often the case, Frantz Fanon (2008) contends that "Understanding something new requires us to be inclined, to be prepared, and demands a new state of mind" (p. 75).

Yet all narratives are by no means equally valuable, equally effective. For Walter Fisher (1987), author of *Human Communication as Narration: Toward a Philosophy of Reason, Value, and Action*, a good narrative must meet two measures: coherence and fidelity. Coherence is the degree to which a story makes sense or holds together. It is found in the structure and organization of the story. Fidelity is the truthfulness or reliability of the story. Does the person reading or listening to the story perceive or experience it to be true?

IV

To view communication from the perspective of narratives is to recognize that no story conveys or lends itself to only one meaning, one interpretation. Diversity is the order of narratives, as all human beings have different experiences and are of different environments and circumstances. In this way, a narrative perspective promotes a democratic and pluralistic sensibility. It compels us to recognize and appreciate that our different narratives matter. Our truths reside within our narratives. Our narratives shape the limits and contours of our truths. Democracy is about making space for narratives that are different from our own. Understanding your truth involves understanding the narrative that situates your truth.

V

To view communication from the perspective of narratives is to be vigilant about our proclivity to narrativize. To narrativize is to cohere—to assume that coherence is possible. In other words, to narrativize is to believe that we can make sense of things and that doing so is both healthy and necessary. But can everything be narrativized, and should everything have a narrative? How do we know when to step away from trying to impose a narrative on something? In fact, what damage do we do when we try to impose a narrative on something that should be left without one? Narrative, writes Roy Scranton (2019), "is the enemy." It is "a trick to seduce the mind into making sense of reality, a way of structuring the unknown that presumes we already know how things will end.... Narrative is how we reassure ourselves everything's going to be ok." Moreover, "narrative is the preferred self-imprisonment of gamblers, sexual predators, professional victims, malignant narcissists, the mainstream media, corporate drones, addicts, the perpetually disappointed, children, bourgeois elites, the benighted masses, the dwindling middle class, ethnonationalists, the hopeful, the innocent, the sinning, the damned. Narrative is the escape room of the soul." In many instances, such is no doubt the case. A narrative can stop us from dealing with what is real and binding, such as the fact that our actions and decisions are destroying the planet. A narrative can also stop us from doing what is morally hard and difficult, such as forgiving those who trespass against us. In such instances, writes Scranton, "Narrative seduces. Narrative misunderstands. Narrative confuses. Narrative lies. Narrative is the enemy." However, on the other hand, writes Scranton, "narrative is inevitable, for without narrative, human existence is absurd." Indeed, without narrative, achieving coherence and making sense of things would be impossible. Human existence, for sure, would be absurd. Thus, the challenge for us is to recognize our proclivity to narrativize and to remain always mindful of the danger of doing so.

VI

To view communication from the perspective of narratives is to appreciate that narratives always have a context, that understanding a narrative involves understanding the context, and that narratives also create and

perpetuate various contexts. However, no context is ever clearly and perfectly defined. Context is subjective, which means that context also demands
context. Further, context has many different dimensions (cultural, racial, political, social, ceremonial, and temporal). So what one person views as the
context can be very different to what another person views as the context. Yet
both must still attend to context to understand a narrative. As Simon Ortiz
(2003) explains about determining the meaning of Native American songs,
"A song is made substantial by its context—its reality—both that which is
there and what is brought about by the song. The context in which the song
is sung or that a prayer song makes possible is what makes a song substantial, gives it the quality of realness. The emotional, cultural, spiritual context
in which we thrive—in that, the song is meaningful. The context has not only
to do with you being physically present, but also with the context of the
mind, how receptive it is, which usually means familiarity with the culture in
which the song is sung" (p. 111).

VII

To view communication from the perspective of narratives is to look at communication ethics from the standpoint of intentionality. What are the motives,
reasons, and passions shaping our narratives? Who benefits from our narratives? Note that in US legal practice, intentionality is no defense for uninten-
tionally presenting a falsehood as fact in court proceedings. However, from a
narrative perspective, intentionality means that communication is also about
determining what the person's intent is. In short, from the perspective of the
person telling the story, the moral of the story is important. From a narrative
perspective, the moral, rather than the facts, of the narrative is what is important. To know the moral of the story is to know the intent of the story.

VIII

To view communication from the perspective of narratives is to view politics
in terms of whose narratives are dominant, what narratives are dominant,
how those narratives are blocking the rise of new narratives, and how other

narratives are resisting these dominant narratives. In other words, the study of politics is about those who wield power by imposing various narratives, and those who resist that power by promoting a different set of narratives. In this regard, to view communication from the perspective of narratives is to understand that there will always be new narratives that aspire to undermine, displace, and delegitimize dominant narratives, and dominant narratives in turn will always aspire to undermine, displace, and delegitimize emergent narratives. Case in point, finding any discussion of the Navajo's story of communication, or that of the Cherokee or any other Native American people in any introductory communications textbook is nearly impossible. But do Native Americans really have nothing important to say about communication? Politics from a narrative perspective is a struggle about what narratives will rule us. For example, every prophet sought to present a new narrative of God that undermined the legitimacy of dominant narratives of God. Yet such initiatives were always met with hostility and persecution. From a narrative perspective, colonialism happens at the narrative level rather than simply at the level of language. How are Indigenous peoples' narratives erased, displaced, and silenced, and other peoples' imposed, legitimized, and celebrated? From a narrative perspective, what should always be of concern to us are those narratives that are never promoted, never endorsed, never memorialized.

As Kathryn Schulz (2016) points out, more than 150 years after the Emancipation Proclamation, there is still no federal monument to the millions of human beings who were enslaved in the United States for over 250 years. Neither is there any kind of national monument for the victims of the 4,000 lynchings that occurred between 1877 and 1950 in the United States. Yet there are countless official markers and monuments to the Confederacy. In this regard, Toni Morrison's words are profound: "There is no place you or I can go, to think about or not think about, to summon the presences of or recollect the absences of slaves. There is no suitable memorial or plaque or wreath or wall or park or skyscraper lobby. There's no three-hundred-foot tower. There's no small bench by the road. There is not even a tree scored, an initial that I can visit or you can visit in Charleston or Savannah or New York or Providence, or, better still, on the banks of Mississippi" (quoted in Denard, 2008, p. 44). The point being that politics from a narrative perspective is most often about the struggle for memory. The narratives that are promoted and memorialized will dictate what memory and whose version of history will prevail.

IX

To view communication from the perspective of narratives is to be vigilant about our own complicity in promoting master narratives. Again, all narratives by no means possess equal power and privilege. Certain narratives are dominant, and others less so. Dominant narratives are often called **master narratives**—the narratives that validate and cultivate the ideological and material interests of elites. Such a narrative succeeds by creating the impression that it represents how the world really is. It does this by masking its ideological origins, meaning its human origins. We are to forget that everything human, like our worldview, reflects our beliefs, values, fears, ambitions, doubts, and suspicions. A master narrative also succeeds by appearing to be fully coherent and devoid of chaos, confusion, and contradiction. Further, a master narrative succeeds by appearing to be equally and objectively serving the interests of all, when such is never the case. Finally, a master narrative succeeds by employing a set of auxiliary apparatuses to maintain its dominance. That human differences (race, gender, sexuality identity, nationality, etc.) are the origins of human problems is a master narrative. This narrative forms the foundation of the claim that communication problems result from the fact that men and women use and experience language differently. It figures prominently in the writings of Deborah Tannen (1990), a professor of linguistics at Georgetown University and author of the bestselling book *You Just Don't Understand: Women and Men in Conversation*. But this popular claim is false, as analysts have demonstrated again and again (Burleson, 1997; Goldsmith & Fulfs, 1999). No doubt, men and women do use and experience language differently. But our communication problems have no origins in such differences, or in any other human differences. Instead, our communication problems most often result from a lack of empathy and compassion, or our unwillingness to be vulnerable to the narratives and perspectives of others. Still, to promote the claim that our communication problems result from our differences is to validate and promote a master narrative that thrives on us being afraid and suspicious of human differences.

X

To view communication from the perspective of narratives is to recognize that worldviews are narratives and thus reflect our limits to understand the world completely and perfectly. No human being is capable of knowing anything absolutely and completely. In the face of this reality, human beings invent fictions, which in turn make for narratives. So at the foundation of every narrative, every worldview, is a fiction or a set of fictions. This makes every narrative and worldview fallible and vulnerable. Case in point, in his book *Clash of Civilizations and the Remaking of World Order*, which was subsequently translated into over 33 languages, Samuel Huntington (1997) warns of a coming Armageddon between the Western/European world and other civilizations. He argues that the West needs to prepare for this coming clash of civilizations by rejecting multiculturalism, bilingualism, and other threats to its ideological stability. After September 11, 2001, the phrase *clash of civilizations* was ubiquitous in the United States. Indeed, reviews of Huntington's books begin with sentences like "Samuel Huntington is one of the most eminent political scientists in the world" (*New York Times*), "Samuel Huntington is a distinguished scholar who always addresses important and timely issues" (*Los Angeles Times*), "In the course of a remarkable distinguished academic career, Samuel Huntington has demonstrated a steadfast commitment to realism" (*Foreign Policy Journal*), "Harvard scholar Samuel Huntington [is] the most important political scientist in America.... When Huntington writes, people listen—or they should" (*National Review*), "Samuel Huntington, of Harvard University, has a knack for giving sharp voice to issues which have drifting inchoate in other people's minds" (*Times-London*), "Samuel Huntington is a professor of Harvard University, a noted scholar and the author of the global bestseller, *The Clash of Civilizations and the Remaking of World Order*" (*The Economist*), and "Samuel Huntington is the author of the most important works of political science of this generation" (*Weekly Standard*).

However, Huntington's ominous warnings are in no way new. People have always been warning about the threat one group of human beings poses to another. It is probably the oldest narrative. Yet it is also the most violent and destructive narrative—there would be no Holocaust without this narrative. What Huntington is giving us is a story of the world. He is no doubt entitled to this story, and all the fictions that come with it. But in the end, this is merely one story, reflecting a certain way of imagining and believing what the world is and can be. Huntington's facts and truths are nothing but creatures of Huntington's narrative, Huntington's worldview. No facts or truths are ever separate or outside of a story. Our narratives frame and situate our facts and truths. This is why to understand any person fully involves understanding that person's narrative, that person's worldview. To understand the person's narrative is to understand why only certain facts and truths appeal to the person. Why is the person unwilling to understand certain things? Thus, from a narrative perspective, what should concern us most are the implications and consequences that come with different narratives, as well as the origins of different narratives. Does this story expand our understanding and experiencing of the world? Where is this story coming from? Why are we creating this story now? What is this story's appeal? Why is this story appealing to us now? To whom is this story appealing to, and why?

XI

To view communication from the perspective of narratives is to challenge the value and importance of truth in achieving social evolution. We generally believe that the pursuit of truth is necessary for progress and our own social evolution. This belief assumes that human beings have the ability to acquire objective truths—that is, to make claims about the world that are outside and separate from time and space. We generally believe that objective truths should be the foundation of our ethics (our understanding of what is right and wrong). In other words, what is right and wrong should reflect what is true and false. However, a narrative perspective assumes that human beings have no capacity to achieve objective truths. There is simply no way for us to escape our beliefs, our values, our ambitions, our fears, our biases, our prejudices. Instead of truth, a narrative perspective contends that our ethics should be derived by examining the implications and consequences of different narratives. For example, which narratives make for less misery and suffering? Thus, rather than truth, our ethics should be based on consequences and implications. We should be about creating compelling narratives that are laden with ambiguity, complexity, and diversity.

Compelling narratives lend for rich interpretations of the world by embracing the world's boundless ambiguity, complexity, and diversity. In contrast, less compelling narratives seek to diminish ambiguity, complexity, and diversity. Put differently, compelling narratives are **open systems**, permeable and vulnerable to new meanings and interpretations. We embody compelling narratives by always listening to all the possible different sides of a story. We never assume that there is merely one side to any story. A narrative perspective assumes that the condition of the world is bound up with the condition of our humanity, with the condition of our narrativity. It would challenge us to look at the relationship between our increasing degradation and destruction of the world's ecological systems (rivers, forests, oceans, wetlands, etc.) with our increasing determination to achieve objective truths, meaning claims about the world that appear to be devoid of ambiguity, complexity, and diversity. In other words, a narrative perspective would suggest that our destruction of the planet's natural ecosystems reflects our hostility to the world's boundless ambiguity, complexity, and diversity.

A narrative perspective assumes that reversing this destructive direction will demand, among many other things, recognizing the dangers of valuing, elevating, and even worshipping only *one* narrative, because no narrative—meaning no human system—can tame or capture the world's boundless ambiguity, complexity, and diversity. To come to terms with this reality is to recognize the fecund nature of the world. The world in no way wishes to limit us to one truth, one meaning, one understanding. Our submission to any one system of truths or meanings is of our own doing.

XII

Finally, to view communication from the perspective of narratives is to believe that human beings have no capacity to objectively (and rationally) process information. The world of *hard* facts and *cold* truths is nothing but an illusion. What we view as a hard fact and a cold truth is a matter of perspective. Yes, gravity is a hard fact, but without it being given meaning by us, this fact means nothing. So without meaning, hard facts and cold truths mean nothing. Further, without a narrative, no meaning can be found for any truth or fact. No truth stands outside of a narrative. To understand a truth involves understanding the narrative that situates that truth. Our meanings also come from our narratives, which means that our narratives will determine what truths matter to us and in what ways. Further, in a world of hard facts and cold truths, communication is impossible. If, after all, one person has such facts and truths, what becomes the incentive for communication? That is, what can communication accomplish when I am fully convinced that I possess the hard facts and the cold truths and the other person has something different? What would be my incentive to listen to you? Where would diversity originate? To view communication from the perspective of narratives is to believe that every narrative (every story) offers a different truth, a different interpretation of how the world is and could be. Of course, truths are by no means morally and ecologically equal. But to know my narrative is to know my truth, and why I value this truth. In promoting communication, narratives promote diversity and democracy. By encouraging us to listen to each other, narratives push us to hear truths and experiences that are different from our own.

Conclusion

Viewing communication from the perspective of narratives highlights human subjectivity. Communication is about our own construction and organization of reality, reflecting our own fears, biases, beliefs, and standpoints. It is our story of reality. When you ask "How was your day?" my response reflects my understanding of what transpired today. It is my story of today. "Today was great. I got an A on my English paper and I met this really attractive person who is a communication major." In this story I am revealing to you what I value. I could have said, "Today was horrible. I did nothing to help the hundreds of millions of people who live on less than two dollars a day." Every narrative has a perspective. In other words, no communication is ever devoid of ideology. My story reflects my ethics and politics. In the first response, my day was great because good things are happening to me. What happens to me is important to me. This shapes my perspective. In the other response, my day was horrible because horrible things are happening to other people. The concerns of other people matter to me. I tend to view the world from the perspective of others. Both responses reflect different perspectives, different politics. Finally, viewing communication from the perspective of narratives brings into focus the notion of coherence. Our narratives aspire to achieve coherence. Our narratives always reflect how things make sense to us. However, in striving to achieve coherence, we omit, twist, and downplay those things that impede or undermine the coherence we desire. There are always illusions, distortions, and fabrications in communication. Nobody is ever telling the complete and absolute truth—for nobody can.

Discussion Questions

I. Your identity is a narrative (your story about who you are) and, as such, is laden with all kinds of fictions, distortions, omissions, and exaggerations. Can you identify in your story of yourself your fictions, distortions, omissions, and exaggerations?

II. If communication is about storytelling, why should any person have the power to determine what narratives are legitimate?

III. What does the narrative perspective reveal to you about how your biases and prejudices help form your impressions and narratives about people, which can often be wrong?

IV. How do you feel about the idea that your narrative about any person is purely a fiction you have made up about that person? That is, your impression of a person is never an objective fact?

V. Why should you be careful about judging and condemning another person?

chapter six

COMMUNICATION AS PERFORMANCES

I

To view communication from the perspective of performances is to view all of life as performances. Oceans moving and tumbling, rivers running and gyrating, trees swaying and dancing, animals roaming and playing, dolphins jumping and prancing, volcanoes erupting and exploding, birds chirping and soaring, winds coming and going, clouds forming and changing, and earthquakes bending and reshaping the planet are all performances. Through movement life finds expression. To use Mark Johnson's (2007) words, found in the book *The Meaning of the Body: Aesthetics of Human Understanding*, "Movement is life." It is "one of the conditions for our sense of what our world is like and who we are" (p. 19). In fact, movement is "one of the principal ways by which we learn the meaning of things and acquire our ever-growing sense of what our world is like" (p. 21). For Raffi Khatchadourian (2018), "The human animal is a creature of movement ... Our sense of self, our sense of others, and the way we formulate ideas are often shaped by the way we move, by the way we expect others to move" (p. 58). In other words, that life is performative means that life is constitutive. It is shaped, nurtured, and expressed through movement.

II

To view communication from the perspective of performances is to assume that human beings are performative beings. We perform our lives. A living being is a performative being. Our life appears through costumes, scenes, scripts, stages, actors, props, and audiences. All of life is a production, with us taking on roles of actors, spectators, creators, costume designers, directors, and producers. Indeed, every communication class is a production, involving a stage where teachers and students take on different roles, follow different scripts, and wear different costumes. As Samuel Heilman (1979) explains, "no activity in which people involve themselves during everyday life can be isolated from the effects of others. Whether one is in the front stage area or the back stage region, one is always on stage. One is either an actor or audience or both, either taking in others with his performance ... or being taken in by one's own performance" (p. 225). Moreover, "the nature of a performed role, one perception of its possibilities and requirements, is regulated by the particular performance within a particular stage setting or context which itself replicates or reflects the assumptions of the universe within which the event occurs" (p. 205). Consequently, "the frames within which one may operate and still make some sense are by no means arbitrarily constructed nor are they independent of other socio-cultural constructions. They are socially determined and bounded" (p. 205). In other words, the size, nature, and importance of the stage will guide what roles are permitted and how roles are defined and performed. So the stages you have access to are important in terms of what roles a society will allow you to embody and what kind of human being you can ultimately become.

III

To view communication from the perspective of performances is to assume that communication is performative. According to Dennis Davis and James Jasinski (1993), "the most basic and common function of communication is performance, not transmission of information. Performance occurs in rituals and other practices used within communities to coordinate experience and induce common perceptions of the social world" (p. 144). To perform communication is to embody communication. Shouting, screaming, singing, gesturing, hollering, dancing, crying, mimicking, ridiculing, mocking, twisting, twirling, finger-snapping, and head-rolling are all elements in our performing of communication. Viewing communication from the perspective of performances begins with the proposition that human beings perform life and everything that relates to life, including communication. Through our performances we give life form, function, and meaning. We therefore do much more than bring narratives to things; we also bring performances to things. In fact, our narratives and performances guide and shape our meaning of things.

IV

To view communication from the perspective of performances is to assume that human beings perform language. That we perform language means that we embody language. How we use and experience language reflect the entirety and complexity of our being. That is, how we use and experience language reflect all the dimensions (biological, social, cultural, ideological, emotional, sensual, intellectual, etc.) of our being. That we embody language helps explain why women and men perform language differently in public spaces. Take the case of bathroom graffiti. On public bathroom walls, the way women use language is fundamentally different to how men use language (Rodriguez, 2015). Compared to the anonymous writings found in men's bathroom stalls, women's bathroom writings are strikingly and consistently less racist, less violent, less derogatory, less profane, less competitive, less threatening, less sexually explicit. Also, women's bathroom writings are more interactive and interpersonal. Women raise serious questions about topics such as love, how to handle sexual relations, and relationships. Also, women's graffiti solicits advice and shares experiences. Neither type of graffiti is found in men's bathrooms. The differences in how women and men anonymously use and experience language in bathroom stalls reminds us that even though sex is biological, gender is "created through communication," meaning that "gender is learned communication behavior" (Nelson, 2016).

V

To view communication from the perspective of performances is to recognize how our society gives us our roles and instructions on how to perform those roles (scripts). Society enforces our roles and scripts through all manner of devices, practices, and arrangements. This includes enforcing certain norms and taboos, and publicly shaming individuals who challenge the definition

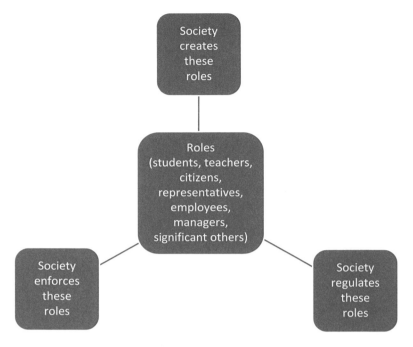

Figure 6.1 Society Creates Our Roles

of certain roles. Finally, society dictates what roles and scripts are tolerable and permissible (see Figure 6.1). It does so by enacting laws banning certain kinds of roles, such as laws banning women from taking on certain roles.

VI

To view communication from the perspective of performances is to view communication problems in term of roles:

- Failure to know your role (e.g., "I am not your friend." "You need to know your place." "I am your mother." "What is wrong with you?")
- Failure to perform your role properly (e.g., "Judge Kavanaugh was rude and hostile. That is no way for a judge to act.")
- Failure to know the rules that come with your role (e.g., "This is no place to be acting like that. I thought you knew better.")

- Failure to know the expectations that come with your role, or failure to conform to the expectations that surround certain roles (e.g., One woman saying to another, "You need to woman up. This is no way for a grown woman to act." Or one man saying to another, "You need to man up. Act like a man.")
- Finally, failure to understand the roles that others play (e.g., "Do you ever stop and think for a moment about all the stuff I have to put up with as a teacher?")

VII

To view communication from the perspective of performances is to assume that impressions matter. The impressions that others form of us are important to us. We care about how others define, perceive, and experience us, especially the first impressions that others form of us. We want the impressions that others form of us to be positive and also of our making. This is the foundation of **impression management theory**, originally formulated by Erving Goffman (1959) in *The Presentation of Self in Everyday Life*. According to this theory, communication is fundamentally about us managing the impressions that others form of us. We use our scripts, our clothes, our actions, our props, our settings, our hairstyles, and our mannerisms to guide and shape the impressions that others form of us. Impressions reflect our identity. In controlling the impressions that others form of us, we are also controlling how others define, engage, and value us. If others view us as competent, trustworthy, and kind, then that positive impression supposedly promises certain benefits and rewards. In short, successfully managing the impressions that others form of us promises various material, professional, social, relational, and financial rewards and benefits.

In *The Evolution of Cooperation*, Robert Axelrod (1984) discusses different ways that a good reputation reduces the cost of doing business in positive ways. A case in point would be lenders charging low rates for credit to people with impressive reputations, versus charging higher fees and rates to those with less impressive reputations to secure the same loans. Impression management is an integral component of **role theory**—human beings are always taking on different roles. It figures prominently in our understanding of a phenomenon found in empirical research called **social desirability bias**—the unwillingness of respondents to share embarrassing information with researchers. It is also proving to be a valuable framework in understanding how people are using social media, such as using enhanced photos and profiles to create positive impressions of themselves for potential employers (Paliszkiewicz & Madra-Sawicka, 2016).

VIII

To view communication from the perspective of performances is to assume that identity is performative. We perform our identities, meaning that our identities are inherently political rather than merely social. That we perform our identities means that our identities are visible, seen in how we move and behave, how we dress and fashion ourselves, and how we design and adorn our spaces. As such, our politics is always on display. We are either at times acting in ways that conform with the roles society has given us, or doing differently. That identity is performative means that much of our politics happens at the level of identity. This can be seen in headlines in the *New York Times* that read, "Behind Quebec's Ban on Face Coverings, a Debate Over Identity," "Why Iranian Women are Taking Off Their Scarves," "I Cross My Legs, Does That Make Me Less of a Man?" "Traditional Dresses as Resistance in Mexico," and "Serena Williams Won't Be Silenced: Her Clothes Are Doing the Talking." That identity is performative means that identity is a site of struggle, either to conform or to resist. No identity is politically neutral. That I identify with a certain group means that I am expected to perform an identity that reflects that group. However, there is never any consensus on what any group identity should be, and thus what the proper performative identity is. Yet there are always people who are determined to impose a certain performative identity on the group, such as demanding that all Muslim women wear burqas, and those who are no less determined to resist.

IX

To view communication from the perspective of performances is to appreciate the importance of play (pretend play, physical play, imaginary play) in human development. Analysts report again and again that pretend play "develops young children's creative thinking" by cultivating various "cognitive and affective processes" that "are important in creativity" (Saracho, 2002, p. 433). In a paper titled "The Importance of Play in Promoting Healthy Child Development and Maintaining Strong Parent–Child Bonds," Kenneth Ginsburg (2007) reports that in children, play promotes "imagination, dexterity, and physical, cognitive, and emotional strength." It is also "important to healthy brain development." Through play, "children at a very early age engage and interact in the world around them." Moreover, play "allows children to create and explore a world they can master, conquering their fears while practicing adult roles." Through this mastery, "play helps children develop new competencies that lead to enhance confidence and the resiliency they will need to face future challenges." Moreover, play "allows children to work in groups, to share, to negotiate, to resolve conflicts, and to learn self-advocacy skills." Finally, play helps children "practice decision-making skills, move at their own pace, discover their own areas of interest, and ultimately engage fully in the passions they wish to pursue" (Ginsburg, 2007). Then there is the play that comes in the form of joking, heckling, teasing, and flirting. This kind of play is important in communication, and even forms the foundation of our civilization (Social Issues Research Center, 2004). It helps manage tensions and conflicts. It also helps in defining relationships, as in "If I am comfortable with you, I can make fun of you." But, most of all, this kind of play allows us to explore different dimensions of ourselves and each other by lessening the anxiety that usually comes with these processes.

X

To view communication from the perspective of performances is to contest the textual (writing) hegemony that shapes common understandings of communication. This hegemony refers to our fixation with viewing communication as a text that is either spoken, written, or visualized. Consequently, the communication that usually matters most to us is that which is spoken, written, and visualized. Thus, what gets erased and devalued is any communication that is neither spoken, written, nor visualized. What also gets erased and devalued are the experiences, knowledges, and struggles found in any communication system that is neither spoken, written, nor visualized. As Dwight

Conquergood (2002) explains, these things "have been erased because they are illegible; they exist, by and large, as active bodies of meaning, outside of books, eluding the forces of inscription that would make them legible, and thereby legitimate" (p. 146). Also erased "is the whole realm of complex, finely nuanced meaning that is embodied, tacit, intoned, gestured, improvised, co-experienced, covert—and all the more deeply meaningful because of its refusal to be spelled out. Dominant epistemologies that link knowing with seeing are not attuned to meanings that are masked, camouflaged, indirect, embedded, or hidden in context" (p. 146).

According to Conquergood, "The visual/verbal bias of Western regimes of knowledge blinds [us] to meanings that are expressed forcefully through intonation, silence, body tension, arched eyebrows, blank stares, and other protective arts of disguise and secrecy" (p. 146). In other words, a visual/verbal bias represents power and privilege: "Subordinate people do not have the privilege of explicitness, the luxury of transparency, the presumptive norm of clear and direct communication, free and open debate on a level playing that the privileged classes take for granted" (p. 146). Consequently, Conquergood believes that the "hegemony of textualism needs to be exposed and undermined. Transcription is not a transparent or politically innocent model for conceptualizing or engaging the world. The root metaphor of the text underpins the supremacy of Western knowledge systems by erasing the vast realm of human knowledge and meaningful action that is unlettered" (p. 147). Paul Gilroy also believes that communication studies now needs to move beyond this "idea and ideology of the text and of textuality as a mode of communication practice which provides a model for all other forms of cognitive exchange and social interaction" to better understand and represent the struggles, knowledges, and experiences of all peoples, especially those who are oppressed, marginalized, and subjugated (quoted in Conquergood, 2002, p. 148).

XI

To view communication from the perspective of performances is to assume that communication is fundamentally a social activity involving actors and spectators rather than an informational activity involving speakers and listeners. In other words, the primary function of communication is social rather than informational or even persuasional. That communication is social means that our performativity emerges through conjoint action. Social also means that my own notion of personhood is socially constituted in situated practice. This means that my intentions, motivations, and actions are shaped and influenced by the intentions, motivations, and actions of others. Social also means that our actions are always being coordinated, and that meaning emerges from coordinated actions. We are always responding to and anticipating each other's actions and decisions. That is, our own actions and decisions are always in response to or in anticipation of the actions and decisions of others. The mistakes that inevitably occur in this process open the possibility for creative action. Thus, social means being in the vortex of converging and diverging forces that create meaning and undermine meaning. Finally, and most importantly, social means that communication is the primary form of experience in which our lives are lived and our relationships and institutions are experienced. In sum, social represents the influences of all the encounters and relationships that make for the formation of our ways of being.

XII

To view communication from the perspective of performances is to assume that the mind dwells in the body, just as much as the body dwells in the mind. A body in motion is a mind in motion. A body in motion also means communication reflects a mind in motion. Whereas other perspectives of communication view communication as a tool that allows us to express what is in our minds, a performance perspective views communication as an expression of mind. Communication shapes and reflects our minds—mind and communication are bound up with each other. Also, that the mind dwells within the body means that the condition of the body always reflects the condition of the mind. A body that is full of passion and vitality reflects a mind that is full of passion and vitality. On the other hand, a body that is in turmoil reflects a mind that is in turmoil. But again, popular perspectives in communication studies assume that the mind is cognitive rather than performative. Supposedly, communication is merely a tool that allows us to express what is in our minds. However, a performance perspective assumes that the mind is in the body. We embody the mind, and the mind is performative rather than merely cognitive. Thus, what is happening with the body now becomes important. The notion that the mind is in the body challenges the dominant view that the mind is cognitive. That the mind is in the body means that communication is also in the body, which means that the body plays an important role in how we perceive, experience, and make sense of the world and each other. It also means that our performativity fleshes out our humanity. Case in point, strenuous physical activity undercuts mental health problems, enhances memory and cognitive functions like decision making, and makes us less susceptible to age-related diseases like dementia and Alzheimer's (Southwick & Charney, 2018). Also, emerging mental health treatments increasingly focus on enhancing positive emotions and decreasing negative thoughts by changing our behaviors rather than merely changing our thoughts and emotions. In short, performativity means that our mental, emotional, existential, and spiritual condition is bound up with our physical condition.

XIII

To view communication from the perspective of performances is to assume that the body is political. How our bodies move and behave is always policed and contested. There are always social, cultural, and political forces pressuring our bodies to conform to arbitrary standards of beauty and decency. Take the case of black women and natural hairstyles (involving no kind of chemical processing). Black women have long faced discrimination for wearing natural hairstyles, such as dreadlocks, braided cornrows, or afros (Campbell, 2019). Such hairstyles are often seen as a violation of a company's grooming policy. US courts also offer no protection for women who face discrimination or job loss for wearing natural hairstyles. In a study investigating implicit bias, "white women showed the strongest bias—both explicit and implicit—against textured hair [natural black hair], rating it as less beautiful and less professional than smooth hair" (Campbell, 2019). That the body is political is also seen in campaigns by women to do what men can legally do in nearly every corner of the world: go topless. Indeed, why should women be deprived of this kind of equality? Also, why should women's bodies be subject to more kinds of policing than men's? That the body is political also means that creativity is also always policed and contested. This is seen in every controversy involving what an artist can legally and socially do. Should Spencer Tunick be allowed to take photos of thousands of nude people in public spaces? Should Renee Cox be allowed to depict Jesus Christ at the Last Supper as a nude black woman? Should Scarlett Johansson be allowed to play a transgendered man? In all these instances, what is being contested is who has the authority to decide and determine what we can experience.

XIV

To view communication from the perspective of performances is to value the power of staging. There is always a stage in communication. However, all stages are by no means politically equal and thus command equal respect and credibility. To view communication from the perspective of performances is to be concerned with how stages are created, constituted, and controlled. Also, who gets access to what stages, and how do various stages control how communication is performed? Power resides in those who control the staging of communication, including who gets access to what stages (platforms) and what audiences.

XV

Finally, to view communication from the perspective of performances is to view power and politics from the standpoint of who determines which roles and performances are legitimate, and by what means, devices, and rationales (see Figure 6.2). Also, what performances are challenging and contesting the legitimacy of dominant performances? Indeed, what happens when various peoples refuse to adopt certain roles and scripts and are even determined to invent new roles and scripts that our society rejects, scorns, and disparages? Moreover, from a performative perspective, politics is about deplatforming—a new form of activism that is about refusing to allow individuals with certain views to have a stage and thus an audience, such as students disrupting talks by certain speakers on college campuses.

Viewing politics from a performance perspective is also about recognizing how expectations that surround certain roles can harm and diminish the humanity of others. Take the case of the US military. The US military has a sexual

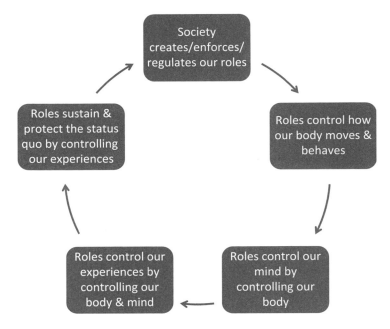

Figure 6.2 The Power of Roles

assault problem. According to the US Department of Defense, there were 20,500 instances of unwanted sexual contact in 2018, an increase of 38 per cent from 2016 (Phillips, 2019). However, the US military often refuses to believe people who report being raped. Ryan Leigh Dostie (2019) contends that the military has a tendency of refusing to take seriously claims by victims who, when being raped, never yelled, screamed, or fought back—that is, never "acted enough 'like a rape victim.'" "It's as if there is a list somewhere about how we, the raped, are supposed to act, how to play our parts for those who will judge us." This disturbing case study reminds us of the need to be vigilant about how we impose our expectations on others by how we situate people in different roles.

Conclusion

To view human beings as performative beings is to end the separation between mind and body. The mind emerges through movement. In this way, our minds will always reflect how boldly and courageously we move in the world. However, there are always scripts that seek to guide and shape how we move in the world. Being a teacher comes with a script. Being a student comes with a script. Being a husband comes with script. Being a wife comes with a script. Being a woman comes with a script. Being a man comes with a script. Being a girlfriend comes with a script. Being a boyfriend comes with a script. Then there is the role that society plays in enforcing those scripts through all kinds of rules, norms, and taboos. The notion of performativity makes a valuable contribution to communication studies by reminding us that the body plays a vital role in shaping how we perceive, experience, and make sense of things. What we are capable of understanding is bound up with what our bodies are doing, who is surrounding and interacting with our bodies, and where our bodies are moving through time and space.

Discussion Questions

 I. In what ways is your own life a performance?
 II. What do you find to be most valuable about the idea that human beings perform communication? How does this idea change the way you look at communication?
 III. If "true philosophy" is "the art of living the good life" (rather than the art of studying the good life), then how could the study of communication become "true philosophy"? In other words, what do you define as "the art of living the good life," especially the "art," the "living," and the "good life"? Also, why do you define these things in the ways you do?
 IV. If the mind is in the body, as much as the body is in the mind, then who should have the power to determine how the body behaves? That is, who should have the power to discipline the body, and ultimately your mind?
 V. How do you see different social, cultural, and political forces conspiring to limit your mind by controlling your body?

chapter seven

COMMUNICATION AS RELATIONSHIPS

I

To view communication from the perspective of relationships is to assume that all of life is inherently relational. Nothing survives or thrives in isolation—everything has a relationship to something. Nothing comes into the world by itself. This relational notion appears prominently in the teachings of the Buddha: "All things depend on all other things for their existence. Take, for example, this leaf in my hand. Earth, water, heat, tree, clouds, sun, time, space—all these elements have enabled this leaf to come into existence. If just one of these elements was missing, the leaf could not exist. All beings, organic and inorganic, rely on the law of [inter]dependent co-arising. The source of one thing is all things" (Hanh, 1991, p. 169). That life is inherently relational therefore means that life's prosperity is also inherently relational. In other words, for any life to flourish, other lives must flourish.

II

To view communication from the perspective of relationships is to assume that human beings are relational beings rather than autonomous beings. Human beings, in being an expression of life, are relational beings. You are a relationship rather than a person. Your own life is constituted and influenced by all manner of forces: your parents deciding to have a child, the love and resources (especially moral and financial) of your family, your historical circumstances (others fighting and dying for the many rights you now enjoy), your experiences with others (your teachers, your friends, your girlfriends/boyfriends providing emotional and intellectual resources), the material resources that others make available to you (e.g., scholarships), and so forth. All these things shape what is real to you and how you understand what is real to you. Indeed, from the perspective of communication as relationships, the mind is relational and ecological. It emerges in our relationship with others. Consequently, quality of mind can be measured in quality of relationships. In other words, who is surrounding you and who you are surrounding yourself with is important in shaping your mind and the limits of your imagination. In short, to view communication from the perspective of relationships is to assume that our own humanity is shaped through our relationships with other human beings. No person becomes human without other human beings. Other human beings shape how we define and experience ourselves. As Kenneth Gergen (2009) notes in *Relational Being: Beyond Self and Community*, "virtually all intelligible action is born, sustained, and/or extinguished within the ongoing process of relationship. From this standpoint there is no isolated self or fully private experience. Rather, we exist in a world of co-constitution. We are always already emerging from relationship" (p. xv). The kind of human being we will become will depend on the kind of human beings that surround us. We depend on other human beings, and other human beings depend on us to become human. Consequently, from a relationship perspective, all human beings inherently have certain obligations to other human beings regarding helping others to become fully human. To help others become fully human is to help ourselves become so.

Indeed, to view communication from the perspective of relationships is to take seriously the notion of **recursivity**—our treatment of others shapes us accordingly. It is compellingly captured in Frederick Douglass's claim that "No man can put a chain about the ankle of his fellow man without at last finding the other end fastened about his own neck" (quoted in Ratcliffe, 2010, p. 237). The reason being that the humanity of both persons is relationally intertwined. We become either the good we do to others or the harm we do to others. Recursivity also explains why analysts are newly discovering why saying "thank you" or writing "thank you" is important. Besides generating positive feelings in the recipients of these messages, saying or writing "thank you" also generates positive emotions in us (Kumar & Epley, 2018). From a relationship perspective, communication is about that which we do to make others feel safe and secure. For Geoffrey Vickers (1984), "The most basic function of human communication is to establish, change or maintain the relationship of the parties" (p. 324). In an essay titled "Communication as Relationality," Celeste Condit (2006) writes, "Communication is a process of relating. This means it is not primarily or essentially a process of transferring information or of disseminating or circulating signs (though these things can be identified as happening within the process of relating). Instead, communication is the weaving and reweaving of visible and invisible four-dimensional webs, which constitute and reconstitute matter and ideation as humans, discourse, and other beings within a dynamic field of many forces" (p. 3).

III

To view communication from the perspective of relationships is to assume that we are always situated within relationships (parent/child, teacher/student, employer/employee, artist/audience, coach/athlete, supervisor/supervisee, sibling/sibling, friend/friend, neighbor/neighbor, partner/partner), and those relationships shape our actions, perceptions, and expectations. Moreover, through relationships we develop and adopt roles, and also assign rules and expectations to those roles. Also, through relationships we acquire values, beliefs, modes of intelligibility, and notions of self and personhood. Consequently, as Sheila McNamee and Kenneth Gergen (1999) explain in "Relational Responsibility: Resources for Sustainable Dialogue," "there is no particular account of reality or the good that can lay claim to transcendent foundations or justifications. Any rationality employed for purposes of justifying a given [action or decision] is itself a move in an ongoing language game. It is a rationality born of a particular tradition of discourse and practice. And when such pronouncements are placed in motion, when they become indefensible statements about what is or must be, they operate to the detriment of alternative ways of life. Thus, attempts to adjudicate conflicts in terms of foundational goods are fraught

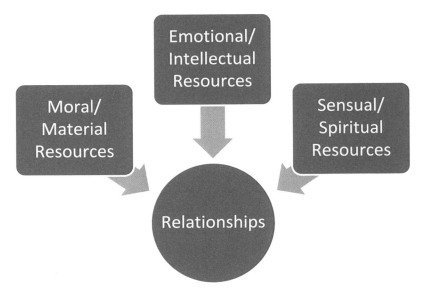

Figure 7.1 Relationships as Resources

with danger.... It also follows that all beliefs about the world and self, about worthy and unworthy, are culturally and historically contingent" (p. 20). Simply put, all forms of intelligibility are relationally contingent. What can make sense in one relationship can make no sense in another.

IV

To view communication from the perspective of relationships is to assume that our relationships either promote our development or undermine our development. That is, our relationships can provide us with all the resources (material, emotional, educational, ideological, spiritual, existential, and communicational) we need to flourish, or deprive us of these resources, and consequently, undermine our flourishing. So all relationships are by no means morally and ecologically equal. From a relationship perspective, our obligation resides in helping others acquire the necessary resources to flourish (see Figure 7.1). Thus, to view communication from the perspective of relationships is to view relationships as resources, which means that quantity, quality, and diversity of relationships are important.

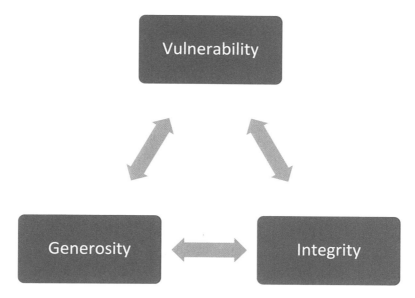

Figure 7.2 Dimensions of Relationships

V

To view communication from the perspective of relationships is to believe that through communication we either are creating and nurturing healthy relationships or undermining and destroying the possibility of such relationships. Relationships are born of communication and consequently perish from a lack of communication. As Deanna Fassett, John Warren, and Keith Nainby (2018) remind us, "Communication is never just a conduit, channel, or tool for transferring information. Communication always produces, makes, and constructs" (p. 15). So when you say positive things to a person ("I enjoyed your class today"), you are simultaneously creating a positive relationship with that person. Indeed, to view communication from the perspective of relationships is to believe that the quality of a relationship is determined by the quality of the communication that shapes that relationship. Empathy, affirmation, and openness are elements of good communication (see Figure 7.2). When our communication is full of these elements, our relationships flourish and blossom. Thus, generosity (to give easily and abundantly of ourselves), vulnerability (to be open to new things and experiences), and integrity (our ability to keep our word) are the measure of all relationships.

VI

To view communication from the perspective of relationships is to believe that a communication problem is ultimately a relationship problem, and relationship problems are fundamentally communication problems. Fixing a relationship problem involves fixing the communication constituting the relationship, which means enriching our communication with empathy, affirmation, and honesty. In fact, disruptions, annoyances, and even wrenching upheavals are common in all relationships because our relationships (or relational history) give us different reference points to know what actions are appropriate. As Sheila McNamee and Kenneth Gergen (1999) explain, "because we bring to bear on any action multiple voices of evaluation (many ways of visioning the true and the good), there is virtually no behavior that cannot be faulted by at least one available standard.... [To] despair of a relationship because of failures of understanding, in achieving mutual agreement, or running smoothly is, to a degree, unwarranted. Such glitches are the normal order of things. From the present standpoint, so-called good understandings are always partial, mutual agreement is precariously situated, and smooth interchange is often just the result of habit. Not every fault demands a culprit" (p. 24). Finally, from the perspective of communication as relationships, communication is solely defined by the individuals constituting the relationship. Anything that promotes a relationship can be defined as communication, just as much as anything that undermines a relationship can be defined as communication. In both cases, "anything" is defined by those in the relationship.

VII

To view communication from the perspective of relationships is to appreciate the value of all relationships, including our relationships with plants and animals. That human beings are relational beings means that all of our relationships matter, meaning that even our relationships to plants and animals can be enriching and rewarding. These relationships also reflect and remind us of the recursive nature of relationships—our treatment of others generates the same sentiments in us. To be kind to a plant is to be kind to ourselves. To be kind to an animal is to be kind to ourselves. Our treatment of others falls back on us. Analysts consistently report that pets can help us reduce tension, anxiety, and even depression (Le Beau Lucchesi, 2017). Petting a dog can improve heart rate, reduce stress hormones, and lower blood pressure in the person petting the dog. Interacting with and taking care of plants also offer many benefits, such as lowering blood pressure, promoting problem solving, reducing stress hormones, lowering levels of anxiety, lessening depression, reducing heart disease, enhancing quality of thinking, and helping patients recover after medical procedures. In sum, all our relationships matter because all relationships have the power to impact our lives.

VIII

To view communication from a relationship perspective is to believe that the study of communication should involve examining how different social, political, ideological, and epistemological forces shape our communication practices and, consequently, shape the limits and contours of our relationships. Put differently, if different relationships come with different resources, which in turn have implications for our development and flourishing, how do different social, political, ideological, and epistemological forces and arrangements ultimately impact what kinds of relationships are available to us? For example, trust is an important element in relationships. In a paper titled "Oxytocin Increases Trust in Humans," Michael Kosfeld, Markus Heinrichs, Paul Zak, Urs Fischbacher, and Ernst Fehr (2005) report that trust "plays a key role in economic exchange and politics. In the absence of trust among trading partners, market transactions break down. In the absence of trust in a country's institutions and leaders, political legitimacy breaks down" (p. 673). Overall, trust "contributes to economic, political, and social success." Kosfeld and company also report that increasing our levels of oxytocin (one of two major hormones secreted from a region of the brain called the posterior pituitary) can cause "a substantial increase in trust among humans, thereby greatly increasing the benefits from social interactions" (p. 673). Specifically, oxytocin affects our "willingness to accept social risks arising through interpersonal interactions." In other words, increasing levels of oxytocin positively changes our perceptions of things and people. However, as much as trust has biological origins in oxytocin, oxytocin levels are influenced by relational and environmental variables. Stress, anxiety, fear, competition, and lack of affirmation impede the release of oxytocin and thereby the rise of trust in relationships. Thus, any society that promotes these kinds of things will obstruct the formation of the kinds of relationships that are vital for our well-being.

IX

To view communication from the perspective of relationships is to believe that politics is about who determines what relationships are legitimate, and thus what kinds of communication are legitimate between human beings. Also, to view communication from the perspective of relationships is to view politics in terms of which practices, structures, and arrangements impede the cultivation and proliferation of all kinds of relationships. Moreover, to view communication from the perspective of relationships is to recognize the value of what political scientists refer to as social capital—the quality and quantity of relationships found in a community. Social capital makes a community efficient. It impedes deviancy and criminality. Also, social capital promotes trust, stability, and continuity. Simply put, social capital vitalizes, lubricates, and binds a community. To view communication in terms of relationships is to challenge the popular claim that human beings are autonomous beings—creators of our own making and doing—and that what is presumably best for us are laws, practices, and arrangements that promote autonomy and self-interest.

X

To view communication from the perspective of relationships is to view the mind as a creation of relationships. Relationships create, nurture, and shape our minds. Knowing my mind involves knowing the relationships that create, influence, and situate my mind. Also, that my mind is relational means that my mind is never fully of my own making. My own mind is born of other minds, which means that my mind is created, nurtured, and shaped by other minds. Consequently, other minds are responsible for the making of my mind. No mind is ever outside or separate from other minds. However, that my mind is born of other minds in no way means that I have no responsibility for my actions and decisions. It merely means that I need to recognize my role in shaping other minds. From the perspective of communication as relationships, ethics is about being conscious of the fact that my mind is always impacting other minds, and other minds are always impacting my mind. What can I do to expand rather than diminish the minds of others, and what can I do to lessen the impact of weak and negative minds on my mind? No mind is ever politically neutral. That minds impact other minds means that minds have consequences. We are always either enriching or diminishing other minds. Thus, communication is a mind-making activity. Through communication we create our minds, and in communication our minds reside. From the perspective of communication as relationships, the study of communication is the study of the mind and all that is bound up with our minds. For what becomes of our minds will ultimately determine what becomes of us. Consequently, knowing what kinds of minds come from different relationships, and the communication that constitutes different kinds of relationships, is important.

XI

To view communication from a relationship perspective is to believe that the quality of our lives comes from the quality, quantity, and diversity of our relationships. For example, longevity and mental health are both related to quantity and quality of relationships (Brody, 2017). Social isolation erodes our mental, physical, and emotional well-being. From the perspective of relationships, the primary mission of communication is to promote social, mental, and psychological wellness. For example, physical affection or positive touching plays a vital role in the mental, emotional, and physical development of human beings. In an article titled "The Magic of Touch," George Howe Colt (1997) reports that positive touching "enhances immune function and lower levels of the stress hormones cortisol and norepinephrine," "lowers anxiety in depressed adolescents," reduces apprehension in burn victims about to have contaminated skin removed, "improves body image in people suffering from eating disorders," and "stimulates the brain to produce endorphins, the body's natural pain suppressors" (p. 60). In fact, there is a positive correlation between increasing levels of physical affection toward infants and children and decreasing levels of deviancy and criminality (Colt, 1997).

Conclusion

We commonly assume that communication happens between human beings. One person is either trying to share something with someone, or trying to persuade someone to do something. However, to view communication from the perspective of relationships is to challenge this assumption and description. The condition of one's humanity is never outside or separate from that of another. How we communicate with others shapes what we become. This claim finds support in what cognitive scientists now refer to as **neuroplasticity**—the ability of the brain to change continuously throughout a person's life. These changes can either be positive or negative, meaning that how we live can either positively or negatively alter the structures and workings of our brains.

Viewing communication from a relationship perspective makes an important contribution to communication studies by expanding our understanding of communication ethics. In communication resides our becoming—as we communicate, so we become. Our becoming is also bound up with the becoming of others. In this way, our relationships always reveal the condition of our humanity. When our relationships are deepening, expanding, and evolving, this reveals a certain kind of communication. Just as good fruit can only come from good trees, good relationships can only come from good communication. In this way, relationships are ecological, which means that communication is no less so. In other words, through communication we create relationships, which in turn provide us with intellectual, emotional, existential, spiritual, and material resources that are vital for our becoming. However, how we embody communication is also shaped by the relationships that nurture us. We create relationships, and then those relationships create us. That communication is ecological—providing us with resources necessary for us to flourish—means that the mission of communication is to promote life through the formation of life-affirming relationships.

Discussion Questions

I. If you were to do a relationship audit of your own life, what would it reveal about how you do communication? (For example, do you help lessen the misery of others, or add to the misery of others?) What communication practices would you want to change?

II. What does social isolation mean to you? How would you define or describe social isolation?

III. How do you see your relationship to your pet or other animals impacting the quality of your life?

IV. How does the notion of relationships being resources alter your understanding of relationships?

V. In what ways can you do relationships better in terms of enhancing the resources you make available to others?

chapter eight

COMMUNICATION AS MODES OF BEING

I

To view communication in terms of modes of being is to view communication as emerging from and reflecting the totality of our being. That is, communication emerges and reflects all the different dimensions of our being (mental, physical, emotional, sensual, cultural, spiritual, existential, and emotional). Communication is about our capacity to share, perceive, and experience. Put differently, communication is about how much we are capable of sharing, perceiving, and understanding. Case in point, in the Bible, Jeremiah (5:21) reads, "Hear this, you foolish and senseless people, who have eyes but do not see, who have ears but do not hear." Matthew (13:14) reads, "You will be ever hearing but never understanding; you will be ever seeing but never perceiving," and Matthew (13:17) reads, "For verily I say unto you, That many prophets and righteous men have desired to see those things which you see, and have NOT seen them, and to hear those things which you hear, and have NOT heard them." These passages speak to the fact that understanding demands and implicates all dimensions of our being. We hear with our minds, our hearts, and our souls rather than merely with our ears. Just as well, we speak with our minds, our hearts, and our souls rather than merely with our mouths. We also see with our minds, our hearts, our souls, rather than merely with our eyes. Many things impede and undermine what we are capable of sharing, perceiving, understanding, and experiencing: our fears, our beliefs, our norms, our biases, our prejudices, our values, our suspicions, our ambitions, and our expectations. This is why communication is about modes of being. What we are capable of sharing, perceiving, understanding, and experiencing is bound up with all of our being. For Mark Sukonik (2016), viewing communication in terms of modes of being is about what you understand "before you attempt to understand. It is the state of mind you have before you open your mind to enter a new one. It is the culmination of your senses, the rhythm of your breath, the frequency of your energy, the body's metabolism, and the health of your mind. It is what you are made of, what you allow to make you, what you are making yourself, and the forces you respond to as you make it" (p. 2). In short, communication is an expression of mind, and mind constitutes the totality of our being.

That communication is an expression of mind also means that mind is developmental rather than merely biological in nature. We can expand the capacity of our minds by pushing against the limits of our own communication—that is, always pushing, challenging, and exercising what we are capable of sharing, perceiving, and understanding. In this way, to view communication from the perspective of modes of being is to view communication as a minding activity. The mind resides in communication. Our communication is either expanding or diminishing our minds. The notion of our mind being bound up with our modes of being is compellingly seen in our emergent understanding of the role of touch in shaping our consciousness of the world and ourselves. That is, who we touch, what we touch, and how many times we touch play a key role in shaping how we perceive and make sense of the world and ourselves. According to Dacher Keltner, a specialist in the science of emotions, "touch is the primary moral experience" and the foundation of all human relationships. It is also, for Keltner, "the social language of our social life" (quoted in Gopnik, 2016). In fact, touch is "the root moral precept of our sense of common humanity." "In the social realm," claims Keltner, "our social awareness is profoundly tactile." For Adam Gopnik (2016), "Our bodies are membranes in the world, with sensations and meaning passing seamlessly through them. Our experience of our bodies—the things they feel, the moves they make, and the textures and people they touch—is our primary experience of our minds.... Grasping, hugging, striking, playing, caressing, reaching, scratching backs, and rubbing rears: these are not primitive forms of communication. They are the fabric of our being conscious. The work of the world is done by handling it. We live by feel." The role of touch in shaping consciousness brings into focus the notion that consciousness is exteriorized—how we live, where we live, and who we live with will shape what we become and can also change what we have become.

II

To view communication as modes of being assumes that we are bound up with each other, which also means that my mind is bound up with your mind. Consequently, our own communication always falls back on us. To be bound up with others also means that we tend to mirror the behaviors of others and adopt the emotional states of those who surround us. For example, children who have depressed parents tend to have higher rates of depression. We mirror the behaviors and adopt the emotional states of others for purposes of **attunement**. Attunement promotes harmony between human beings by allowing us to feel and know what others are feeling and knowing. It lessens discord and conflict. Psychologists refer to this phenomenon of mirroring others as **emotional contagion**—our emotions and behaviors directly shaping the emotions and behaviors of others in similar ways. It reminds us that our minds are shaped and influenced by the actions of others.

Imitation also plays an important role in shaping our minds. It begins in the first days of life and persists throughout our life. According to Steven Southwick and Dennis Charney (2018), authors of *Resilience: The Science of Mastering Life's Greatest Challenges*, imitation "plays an essential role in acquiring behaviors, skills, mannerisms, social bonds, empathy, morality, cultural traditions, and even language" (p. 169). Further, social support—specifically the quantity and quality of our friendships—shapes how we perceive and engage with things. For example, being with a friend, or thinking of one, can change how we perceive a challenge, like climbing a hill. According to Sian Beilock (2015), "people judge hills as less steep and difficult to traverse when they are accompanied by a friend.... The longer you have known the person, the closer you are, and the greater the interpersonal warmth, the more being next to her or just thinking of her lessens the impact of the hill" (p. 225). However, "When you think about someone toward whom you feel ambivalent, you will see the hill as steep and treacherous to climb" (p. 225). Moreover, social support affects our moods and predispositions. Being surrounded by

people with positive predispositions impacts our own moods and predispositions. Finally, social support affects our biology and physiology. For example,
social support is a key factor in how quickly people recover from major sur-
gery. In short, the people who surround us and who we surround ourselves
with shape and influence how we relate to and perceive things.

The notion of one person's humanity being bound up in the humanity of
others is nicely captured in a concept found in South Africa called *ubuntu*.
According to Michael Onyebuchi Eze (2010), the notion of a person becoming
human only through other people "strikes an affirmation of one's humanity
through recognition of an 'other' in his or her uniqueness and difference. It is a
demand for a creative intersubjective formation in which the 'other' becomes a
mirror (but only a mirror) for my subjectivity. This idealism suggests to us that
humanity is not embedded in my person solely as an individual; my humanity is co-substantively bestowed upon the other and me. Humanity is a quality
we owe to each other. We create each other and need to sustain this otherness
creation. And if we belong to each other, we participate in our creations: we
are because you are, and since you are, definitely I am" (pp. 190–91).

III

To view communication as modes of being assumes that we are bound up
with our environments, which also means that our minds are shaped and
influenced by our environments. The organization of space and place influences how we relate to and communicate with others. For example, there is
an important relationship between mental health and urbanization. People
who live in urban areas tend to have higher levels of mental illness than those
who live in rural areas. Also, there is a positive relationship between spatial
proximity and psychological intimacy. Being physically close to someone affects how we treat that person. As Sian Beilock (2015) notes, "We understand
others, and relate to others, in part by how close we are to them physically.
Physical distance information is actually built into the design of the human
brain. The computation of information about how close we are to a looming
threat shifts from the frontal cortex to more rudimentary, pain-related regions
toward the middle of the brain as we get nearer to a possible danger. When
we are in close physical proximity to someone or something, our brain's more

primitive emotional regions perk up, which could help us better understand what others are feeling. A close physical distance paves the way for a strong emotional connection, while greater distance capitalizes on the association we have between distance and disconnection" (pp. 162–63). Moreover, our being bound up in our environments means that the location of the sun and the moon affects our moods and behaviors. For example, there is an important relationship between changing temperatures and deviancy. In sum, the notion that space and place play an important role in shaping and influencing the workings of our mind figures prominently in many cultures. It is found in the philosophy of *feng shui*, developed in China over 3,000 years ago. Feng shui is a philosophy that teaches how to harmonize the energy in an environment to assure good fortune for those inhabiting that space and place. *Feng* means wind, and *shui* means water. According to analysts, "In Chinese culture wind and water are associated with good health, thus good feng shui means good fortune, while bad feng shui means bad luck, or misfortune. Feng shui is based on the Taoist vision and understanding of nature, particularly on the idea that the land is alive and filled with Chi, or energy" ("Six Chinese Cities with the Best Feng Shui," 2013). The Dogon people of Mali, a country in West Africa, also value the relationship between place and communication. A *toguna* is a meeting house normally located in the center of a Dogon village. It is where community elders meet to address the affairs of the community. Togunas have low roofs to force visitors to sit rather than stand. The purpose of this low roof design is to stop participants from standing and becoming animated during discussions. In this way, the design is purposely meant to promote calm discussion and deliberation.

IV

To view communication as modes of being assumes that we are bound up with the world, which also means that our minds are shaped by the condition of our worlds. All human beings have a relationship to the world, and that relationship impacts how we relate, perceive, and make sense of things. Indeed, to view communication from the perspective of modes of being is to recognize that the world's boundless ambiguity forces all human beings to form various beliefs about how the world is and should be. These foundational beliefs shape what we value and how we perceive, experience, and make sense of things. In short, these foundational beliefs shape and influence everything, including how we communicate, why we communicate, and whom and what we communicate with. To be human is to believe, and what we believe matters. That the world forces us to believe should remind us that we will never achieve dominion over the world. To believe is to be fallible. Our communication will always reflect our fallibility. However, to believe is a beautiful thing. It makes "a crack in everything," and this "is how the light gets in" (Leonard Cohen). In short, the world is in peril *not* because we believe, but rather because of what we *choose* to believe.

That we are bound up with the world also means that we must live by the world's rules and rhythms. Regardless of our determination to do otherwise, nothing will lend itself to one meaning, one understanding, or one anything. We will never achieve that kind of certainty and homogeneity. Certainty ends diversity by making communication impossible. As Geoffrey Vickers (1987) observes, language "is creative only because it is imprecise" (p. 105). In a world of boundless ambiguity, the best we can do is invite, deliberate, and approximate. To engage communication in this dialogic way is to embrace our fallibility. Through communication we grapple with the world's boundless ambiguity and shape ourselves and our worlds in doing so. Thus from the perspective of communication as modes of being, the challenge is to devise and promote the most expansive ways of grappling with the world's boundless ambiguity. Put differently, which ways promote the most possibility?

V

To view communication as modes of being assumes that the primary function of communication is developmental rather than informational or persuasional. We become what we communicate and how others communicate to us, which means that our becoming is what really matters. In other words, the measure of communication can be found in our increasing openness to new things and our willingness to be influenced by new things. We become new by being willing to be born anew. As such, communication demands a willingness to die. To understand new things, we must be ready to abandon other things. Such is the order of the world: The old must make way for the new.

This is how life flourishes; this is how communication flourishes. Through communication we become anew by being willing to understand new things.

VI

To view communication from the perspective of modes of being assumes that *communication is about what you are willing to share, what you are willing to believe, and what you are willing to experience*—that is, what do you have the courage to be vulnerable to? Thus, to view communication from the perspective of modes of being is to view communication in terms of vulnerability. Communication is about being vulnerable to everything and everyone. It is about enlarging what we are capable of perceiving, understanding, and experiencing. Definitionally, communication is the habits and practices by which we become vulnerable to the humanity of others. In this way, communication is about removing and releasing ourselves from the fears, suspicions, beliefs, and values that obstruct and limit what we are capable of perceiving, understanding, and experiencing. In short, to view communication from the perspective of modes of being is to believe that vulnerability is the measure of the human experience. How vulnerable we are capable of being and becoming will determine what becomes of us, which means that communication is the measure of our redemption. *As we communicate, so we become*. Indeed, to view communication from the perspective of modes of being is to recognize that understanding reflects a set of attributes. Besides vulnerability, understanding involves humility, generosity, and cognitive complexity. Humility is about embracing our fallibility—we are only capable of understanding so much. In the words of Kendrick Lamar, "Be humble." Something that makes no sense to you can make complete sense to others. Generosity is about assuming the best in others and giving others the benefit of the doubt. It is about refraining from attributing falsehoods and bad intentions to others. Cognitive complexity reflects our tolerance for ambiguity. It is about our threshold for confusion. High levels of cognitive complexity allow us to be patient, to wait for an understanding to unfold on its own terms and conditions. It saves us from rushing to conclusions and dogmatically imposing our perspectives on things. High levels of cognitive complexity allow us to admit, "This is merely my perspective. I could be wrong."

VII

To view communication from the perspective of modes of being is to recognize that different civilizations have fundamentally different conceptualizations of communication that reflect different ambitions and aspirations. Case in point, Hinduism values intrapersonal communication rather than interpersonal communication. Intrapersonal communication is the communication that happens within us. Hinduism assumes that reality is indivisible and inseparable, and thus all notions of division and separation—like that between senders and receivers, encoders and decoders, speakers and listeners, presenters and audiences—are distortions and misrepresentations of reality. So to bring about any kind of change, as Tulsi Saral (1983) explains, "one need not go out and attempt to influence, manipulate, or change others" (p. 55). Instead, "All one needs to be doing is to facilitate an ongoing process of intrapersonal communication. As one begins to acknowledge and communicate with different parts and/or selves of oneself, the external structures begin to dissolve and reform into different patterns of relationships reflecting the existing status of one's internal structures. This highlights the critical need and value of one's ongoing communication with oneself and accounts for the Upanishadic view that ultimate reality is best comprehended through meditative insight into the nature of one's own self" (p. 55).

Hinduism also values transpersonal communication, which assumes a realm of communication beyond our five physical senses, as in two people communicating without using any of these senses. Hinduism assumes that the "limitations of one's physical senses ... limit the perception, cognition, and experience of one's reality" (Saral, 1983, p. 55). The "limitations of the senses tend to become the limitations of the human mind," thereby impeding, distorting, and limiting what we can perceive, communicate, and experience. As such, the goal of communication in Hinduism is to get us beyond our physical senses to help us recognize always that reality is indivisible. Taoism also promotes a conceptualization of communication that is fundamentally different to that found in the Western/European world. In Taoism, communication is about discouraging talk. The *Tao Te Ching*, which represents key teachings in Taoism, has many passages that warn against talk ("More words count less"; "To talk little is natural"; "Those who know do not talk. Those who talk do not know"; "Keep your mouth shut, Guard your senses, And life is full.

Open your mouth, Always be busy, And life is beyond hope"). In Taoism, as Lyall Crawford (1996) explains, talking less is about refraining from imposing "our will, our values, and our opinions on the persons we encounter" so that new things can become possible in our communication with them. "Such a position welcomes the possibility of being changed by what we express and experience with one another. Conversation becomes more meaningful and enjoyable when points of view are relaxed, when personal reputations are deemed irrelevant, and when our attachments to certain ideas are considered less important than the conversation itself" (p. 30). Taoism also views less talking as being vital to undermining systems of power and privilege that suppress human diversity through the abuse and misuse of talk. For if, as Crawford explains, "knowledge is related to power, and if too much talk is not an indication of knowledge, then talking as if one knows is a deceit and an abuse of power" (p. 30). Ultimately, Taoism is about engaging communication as a place of contemplation rather than persuasion.

VIII

To view communication from the perspective of modes of being is to oppose the notion that persuasion is and should be the mission of communication. Richard Perloff (2003), author of *The Dynamics of Persuasion: Communication and Attitudes in the 21st Century*, defines persuasion "as a symbolic process in which communicators try to convince other people to change their attitudes or behavior regarding an issue through the transmission of a message, in an atmosphere of free choice" (p. 8). An important component in this definition is that "persuasion does involve a deliberate attempt to influence another person. The persuader must intend to change another individual's attitude or behavior, and must be aware (at least at some level) that she is trying to accomplish this task" (p. 9). However, according to Perloff, no persuader can make us do something we are unwilling to do. Instead, "People persuade themselves to change attitudes or behavior" (p. 10). In other words, all persuasion is self-persuasion. As Joel Whalen (1996) explains, "You can't force people to be persuaded—you can only activate their desire and show them the logic behind your ideas.... Their devotion and total commitment to an idea come only when they fully understand and buy in with their total being" (p. 50). However, as much as this is the case, persuasion is still about people constantly trying to change our opinions, attitudes, and behaviors without our consent.

For Sally Miller Gearhart (1979), this is a problem. According to Gearhart, "any intent to persuade is an act of violence" (p. 195). The "act of violence is in the *intention* to change another" (p. 196). Gearhart refers to persuasion as "the conquest model of human interaction," as the goal is to impose either our reality, our truth, or our meaning on the other person to change them in ways that conform to our interests and liking. For Gearhart, persuasion violates the integrity of the person, as no consent was given by them to be subject to this process of conquest. Instead, Gearhart believes that "Communication can be a deliberate creation or co-creation of an atmosphere in which people or things, if and only if they have the internal basis for change, may change themselves" (p. 198). In this model of communication, "persons entering the interaction would be certain (1) that no intent to enlighten or to persuade would be made but rather that each party would seek to contribute to an atmosphere in which change for both/all parties can be taken; (2) that there are differences [and genuine disagreements] among those who participate; (3) that though there are differences [and disagreements], the persons involved feel equal in power to each other; (4) that communication is a difficult achievement, something to be worked at, since the odds are great that moments of miscommunication will outnumber moments of communication; [and] (5) that each participant is willing on the deepest level to yield her/his position entirely to the other(s)" (pp. 198–99). Ultimately, communication is about creating a womb where growth can occur by generating, nurturing, and exploring new meanings.

IX

To view communication from the perspective of modes of being assumes that communication problems are problems of egotism and **narcissism** (an obsession with ourselves to the point of making empathy and compassion impossible). Such a reality can be found in comments like, "You are only hearing what you want to hear." Narcissism undermines communication by blocking our ability to understand and experience the world from the perspective of others (empathy and compassion). In other words, narcissism undermines the intellectual, emotional, and spiritual generosity that is vital for the flourishing of communication. It makes us selfish rather than selfless. Yet the consequences of this selfishness always fall back on us since empathy and compassion save us from all manner of mental health struggles, including anxiety and depression. In the end, communication demands a willingness to be vulnerable to things that are even hostile to our own understandings of things. Vulnerability is about generosity—the ability to be selfless for the sake of mutual understanding. Examples of generosity in communication include (1) giving others the time and space to be heard, (2) affirming the positions of others, (3) refraining from condemning and prejudging, (4) trying to understand the circumstances and experiences that make for different viewpoints, and (5) refraining from dehumanizing others by employing dehumanizing language and symbols.

X

To view communication from the perspective of modes of being is to view communication competency in terms of mental, emotional, existential, and spiritual strength. This includes (1) the strength to resist meeting evil with evil, and thereby never using our words to harm and destroy; (2) the strength to do that which is difficult, like forgiving those who egregiously wrong us; (3) the strength to love in the face of hate; (4) the strength to suspend and open to scrutiny all that we believe and value; (5) the strength to change and evolve; (6) the strength to hear what we are unwilling to hear; and, finally, (7) the strength to openly acknowledge our own tribulations, frustrations, and confusions that often make communication impossible. In short, vulnerability reflects strength. If communication is about being vulnerable to the humanity of others, then communication is also about forging the strength (courage and resolve) to do so. How vulnerable we are capable of being is about how mentally, emotionally, existentially, and spiritually strong we are capable of being. In being vulnerable we become strong, and in becoming strong we change how we relate and communicate with others. So why is the study of communication important? Only through communication do we acquire the strength to change, evolve, and become anew. Communication is a human-making process and also a world-making process. Communication is the womb of possibility.

XI

To view communication from the perspective of modes of being is to view communion as the mission of communication. That is, the primary mission of communication is to allow us to experience each other fully and honestly, without any threat of humiliation or retribution. We achieve communion by being completely vulnerable to each other. So rather than viewing communication in terms of sharing, informing, and persuading, to view communication in terms of modes of being is to view communication in terms of vulnerability. Communication begins in our being vulnerable to each other, which in turn demands our being vulnerable to ourselves. The challenge of communication is to enlarge what we are capable of understanding, experiencing, and perceiving.

XII

Finally, to view communication from the perspective of modes of being is to view politics in terms of promoting and encouraging understanding, especially our understanding of those people who stridently and vehemently oppose our values, our beliefs, our principles, and even our truths. The goal of this politics is to lessen division, aggression, confrontation, and ultimately any kind of dehumanization of our opponents. To view communication from the perspective of modes of being is to view communication in terms of understanding, which means that communication is about *what* and *who* we have the capacity or willingness to understand. What you are capable of understanding will be shaped and influenced by what is in your mind, your heart, and your soul. Moreover, your relationships with others, with your environment, and with the world will shape and influence what you understand and what you are capable of understanding. The reason being that the mind is relational, ecological, and spiritual (reflecting our foundational beliefs about the world). Understanding is a humanizing activity. Understanding assumes that the other person matters, and thus is deserving of all the effort that is necessary to be understood.

No doubt, understanding is difficult—sometimes impossible—even after the most strenuous of efforts on our part. Shouting, screaming, cursing, and fussing reflect our own frustration and desperation with achieving understanding. There are also probably limits as to who and what we are capable of and willing to understand. Who, for instance, could understand how a person could enslave another? Still, this perspective (communication as modes of being) pushes us to look honestly and transparently at our own limits of who and what we are capable of or willing to understand. As Alphonso Lingis (1994) reminds us, "To speak in order to establish one's own rightness is to speak in order to silence the other" (p. 71). So even when our opponent is publicly cast as a racist and misogynist (even when rightly so), our focus will always be on engaging and understanding our opponent, doing our utmost to stop any dehumanization of them. Further, when our opponent is cast as evil, or represents all that is evil, then the suggestion is that the people who support our opponent are evil or are ignorantly complicit in promoting evil. However, this creates a destructive reality between good (us) and evil (them) that makes communication impossible and violence almost inevitable.

Conclusion

To view communication from the perspective of modes of being is to view communication in terms of generosity and vulnerability. Who are we capable of becoming vulnerable to, and how vulnerable are we capable of becoming? Also, how much time, space, patience, and tolerance are we capable of extending to others? This emergent perspective makes an important contribution to communication studies by highlighting how communication is bound up with our worldviews. Enlarging what we are capable of sharing, understanding, and experiencing involves surfacing and disrupting the forces and structures that shape how we perceive, experience, and make sense of things. Indeed, our worldview shapes the totality of our being. There can be no attending to communication without also attending to the worldview that situates us in the world. As such, recognizing the forces and structures that limit what we are capable of sharing, understanding, and experiencing is important. Communication is about attending to the limits of what we imagine and perceive to be impossible. To view communication from the perspective of modes of being is to view communication as the womb of possibility, even the possibility of a world without war, poverty, and misery.

Discussion Questions

I. How would you describe your own modes of being? Do you bring a positive or negative energy to others? Do you bring hope or despair? Are you generous and charitable in your judgment of others? Do you assume the worse or best in others? Do you tend to put a smile on the face of others? Is your life full of gratitude?

II. Do you believe there is an increasing decline in empathy? How might you see this decline around you? How might you see this impacting you?

III. How would you describe your own levels of empathy? Does your level of empathy promote or undermine communication? How would others describe your levels of empathy?

IV. What impedes your willingness to understand? Indeed, what can you do to expand what you are willing to understand?

V. What are the limits of your understanding? That is, who and what are you simply unwilling to understand?

chapter nine

INTEGRATION AND DISCUSSION

The goal of this book is to help us understand why the study of communication is important. Individually and collectively, the different perspectives found in this book—communication as *language and symbols*, communication as *messages*, communication as *media*, communication as *meanings*, communication as *narratives*, communication as *performances*, communication as *relationships*, and communication as *modes of being*—make this case. These different perspectives give us different ways of looking at the mission of communication. Communication can function informationally, socially, relationally, developmentally, and ecologically. In other words, human beings do many things with communication. We use communication to shape and define personal, social, and familial relationships. We create identities, societies, and communities with communication. We also innovate and share knowledge through communication. But, most importantly, we make sense of the world and our lives through communication. Finally, every perspective represents different ways of describing and presenting what it means to study communication:

  I. From the perspective of language and symbols, "I study how human beings use language and symbols to achieve different goals and objectives."
 II. From the perspective of messages, "I study how human beings employ messages to meet the needs and demands of different audiences."
III. From the perspective of media, "I study how different social technologies make for different kinds of communication practices and ways of being in the world."

IV. From the perspective of meanings, "I study the relationship between communication and social, political, and ideological systems, specifically how these systems make for different kinds of meanings."

V. From the perspective of narratives, "I study how human beings use narratives to perceive, experience, and make sense of the world."

VI. From the perspectives of performances, "I study how human beings embody and encounter the world as performative beings."

VII. From the study of relationships, "I study how different communication practices give rise to different kinds of social, political, and institutional relationships."

VIII. From the perspective of modes of being, "I study how different kinds of practices and arrangements either expand or limit what human beings are capable of understanding."

Every communication perspective in this book also presents us with a different view of the human experience that shows us possessing many different dimensions. Indeed, to reduce communication to one thing reduces us to one thing. We also learn from all the perspectives that communication plays a vital role in shaping our conceptions of ourselves, the world, and each other. Communication can expand and enrich these conceptions or limit and diminish them. In this regard the study of communication is important because the consequences and implications that come with communication are profound. These consequences and implications are ethical, political, psychological, social, spiritual, existential, and ecological. In other words, these consequences and implications bear upon all dimensions of our humanity. *As we communicate so we become, and as we become so we communicate.*

Knowing and appreciating the different consequences and implications that come with different ways of defining and experiencing communication are vital to understanding why the study of communication is important. Consequently, the study of communication should involve our knowing how to control what consequences and implications we set in motion and are complicit in setting in motion. That is, the study of communication should involve our knowing and recognizing what kind of communication practices make for what consequences and implications. What becomes of ourselves and our worlds by how we engage with and experience communication?

There are also important differences between the different perspectives of communication. Case in point, the different perspectives have different notions of what it means to be communicatively competent. Certain perspectives demand clarity and agreement, whereas others demand generosity and vulnerability. Every perspective of communication also represents a different politics.

I. To view communication from the perspective of language and symbols is to be of a politics that is about what language should rule us and by whose rules.

II. To view communication from the perspective of messages is to be of a politics that is about who controls the creation, configuration, and dissemination of what messages, and who seeks to resist and disrupt these processes and by what means.

III. To view communication from the perspective of media is to be of a politics that is about who controls the medium or the technology.

IV. To view communication from the perspective of meanings is to be of a politics that is about who determines the meaning of things, and who is seeking to disrupt those meanings and by what means.

V. To view communication from the perspective of narratives is to be about a politics that is about who determines what narratives are legitimate, and what narratives are contesting the hegemony of other narratives.

VI. To view communication from the perspective of performances is to be about a politics that is about who determines what performances are legitimate.

VII. To view communication from the perspective of relationships is to be of a politics that is about who determines what relationships are legitimate, and thus what kinds of communication are legitimate.

VIII. Finally, to view communication from the perspective of modes of being is to be of a politics that is about identifying and contesting the forces and arrangements that limit what we are capable of perceiving, experiencing, and understanding.

That the different perspectives of communication make for different politics ultimately means that the different perspectives make for different social worlds (see Figure 9.1). In other words, every perspective invites us to ask, "What kind of world do you want to live in?" In your social world, how

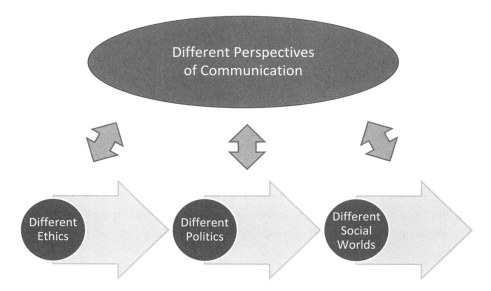

Figure 9.1 Different Perspectives Mean Different Implications

would you want to relate to and communicate with people who hold views and beliefs that are contrary to yours? What would be communicatively tolerable and permissible? Simply put, what would become of difference in your social world? What also of justice? How would justice be communicatively adjudicated in your social world? Which perspective would nurture and promote the kind of justice that complements your social world? In the end, the fact that different perspectives reflect different social worlds reminds us that these different perspectives come with different implications. If there will be no making of a *better* world without *better* communication, then our own notion of a *better* world is bound up with our own understanding of what is *better* communication.

Further, the different communication perspectives define communication problems in different ways and as arising from different places.

I. From the perspective of communication as language and symbols, communication problems arise from our failure to use language and symbols correctly, effectively, and persuasively.

II. From the perspective of communication as messages, communication problems arise from our failure to remove noise from our messages.

III. From the perspective of communication as media, communication problems arise from our failure to use the correct medium to convey our message, or our failure to use our chosen medium properly.

IV. From the perspective of communication as meanings, communication problems arise from our failure to interpret correctly the words and actions of others.

V. From the perspective of communication as performances, communication problems arise from our failure to embody communication in ways that conform to prevailing norms, customs, and expectations.

VI. From the perspective of communication as narratives, communication problems arise from either our failure to cultivate a coherent narrative or our failure to recognize the narrative situating another person's truths.

VII. From the perspective of communication as relationships, communication problems arise from our failure to exercise enough affirmation and compassion.

VIII. From the perspective of communication as modes of being, communication problems arise from our failure to understand the struggles, experiences, and perspectives of others.

Finally, the different perspectives of communication differ in regards to defining and locating the notion of mind. Certain perspectives view communication as a means that allows us to express what is on our minds. Communication expresses the mind. We supposedly use communication to share what is in (or on) our mind. We assume that our minds are outside of and separate from communication. We also assume that our minds are born of our biology. So biology supposedly shows us how the mind works, psychology shows us how the mind behaves, sociology shows us how the mind and society impact each other, anthropology shows us how the mind has evolved over time and space, and communicology shows us what is in (or on) our minds. However, other perspectives of communication view the mind as a creature of communication. Communication constitutes the mind; thus, the mind is born of communication and communication is born of the mind. Through communication we are either pushing and expanding our minds and that of each other, or limiting and diminishing our minds and that of each other. We push and expand each other's minds by pushing and challenging our own minds. We specifically do so by living honestly and transparently, as in being unafraid to openly own our fears, doubts, confusions, and tribulations.

Dialogue and Monologue

Human beings are born into a world of boundless ambiguity. This ambiguity pervades everything—we will never conquer this ambiguity. There will always be questions that will never have answers. For example, who made God? What are the origins of the forces that set off the Big Bang? Moreover, no human being is ever outside of or separate from this ambiguity. Our humanity is shaped against this ambiguity, which means how we relate to this boundless ambiguity will determine what becomes of our lives and our worlds. This is what happens in communication and what communication reflects and captures. Our different ways of embodying and experiencing communication show us either respecting and embracing this boundless ambiguity or disrespecting and seeking to vanquish it. In other words, we can engage this ambiguity from either a dialogic stance or monologic stance.

A dialogic stance reflects our respecting and embracing this ambiguity (see Figure 9.2). When communication is dialogic, the focus is on what is present as well as what is absent. That is, what is never spoken, written, shared, or languaged is no less important than what is spoken, written, shared, and languaged. In a dialogic stance we are always open to the possibility of something new—as in a new interpretation, a new revelation, a new meaning, a new understanding—emerging out of the world's boundless ambiguity. This is also how a dialogic stance cultivates a democratic and pluralistic sensibility. We are always vulnerable to other truths, other perspectives, other understandings. We recognize that we are merely one human being on a planet with billions of other human beings. Our truths are only our truths—there are always other truths.

A monologic stance aspires to limit and vanquish ambiguity (see Figure 9.3). The goal is to rid the world of ambiguity by ridding communication of ambiguity. A monologic stance aims to cultivate and institutionalize one truth, one meaning, or one understanding by removing ambiguity and suppressing conflict. Promoting speech codes or blasphemy laws reflects a monologic

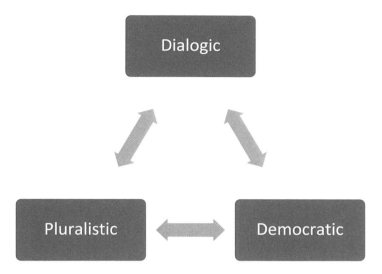

Figure 9.2 A Dialogic Model of Communication

stance. So too does employing various communication devices to suppress the open expression of conflict and dissent in the name of promoting civility and even diversity. Without ambiguity, diversity is impossible. In fact, any determination to end ambiguity makes us autocratic and ethnocentric, undermining our ability to engage and tolerate different truths, different meanings, different perspectives. When communication is impossible, diversity vanquishes.

A dialogic stance recognizes that language is bound up with ideology, which means that any language community is always favoring and cultivating a certain rationality, sensibility, and modality. In other words, every language community is always promoting a certain way of understanding and experiencing the world that favors certain people, interests, and arrangements. What this also means is that every language community has norms and rules that make diversity and the open expression of conflict difficult. To put this differently, nearly every language community has rules and norms that maintain a certain social, political, and epistemological order. However, to achieve new ways of understanding and experiencing things, or to disrupt the status quo, the rules and norms that surround any dominant language community need to be violated, which also means presenting a new sensibility, rationality, and modality in ways that may excite or agitate the violent instincts and impulses

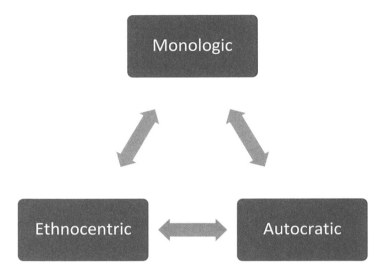

Figure 9.3 A Monologic Model of Communication

of others. In this way, a dialogic stance will always challenge the rules, norms, and idioms that govern any language of power and privilege. Doing so is vital for the entry of new ways of understanding and experiencing things.

Ultimately, a dialogic stance aspires to impede any system of beliefs, values, and practices that suppresses dissent, diversity, and conflict. This is because a dialogic stance assumes that conflict is both natural and necessary. After all, what would become of life's vitality without storms, hurricanes, tornadoes, earthquakes, volcanoes, and forest fires? How would life flourish without these seemingly violent and disruptive forces? Conflict, dissent, and diversity challenge us to look at ourselves anew by challenging our beliefs, values, and fears. This is how these forces play an integral role in our flourishing.

Recognizing the diversity of perspectives that comes with communication is important. Recognizing the virtues and limits that come with different perspectives is also important. However, most important is recognizing that there shall be no better world without better communication. In fact, there will be no better relationship, no better community, no better anything without better communication.

chapter ten

CHALLENGES FACING THE STUDY
AND PRACTICE OF COMMUNICATION

This book began with the premise that the study of communication is important. However, realizing the full potentiality of communication is going to be difficult, as the challenges are many. We can pose these challenges in the form of questions.

I. What becomes of the possibility of communication when we tend to respond negatively and often aggressively to any new information that challenges our view of or belief in something?

II. What becomes of the possibility of communication in a world with less and less empathy and compassion? By any measure, empathy (looking at the world from the perspective of others) is foundational to communication. Thus, what becomes of the possibility of communication in an age of apathy and narcissism?

III. What becomes of communication in a society that is increasingly mediated, saturated, and obsessed with technology? That is, how will the rise of new kinds of technology change the doing of communication and, consequently, the implications and consequences that come with communication?

IV. What becomes of communication in a world that is running out of natural resources and facing ecological peril? That is, as the world's population increases and natural resources diminish, what becomes of communication in the face of such desperation? How much patience and tolerance can those who are thirsty and hungry be capable of mustering?

V. What becomes of the promise of communication in a world full of weapons of mass destruction? That is, how does the proliferation of weapons of mass destruction impact communication between nations with such weapons when conflicting interests arise?

VI. What becomes of the promise of communication against forces, trends, and movements (speech codes, microaggression campaigns, university language covenants, trigger warnings, heresy and blasphemy laws, and inclusive language campaigns) that aim to limit communication for the sake of one reason or another? What becomes of the vitality of communication in the face of these trends? What becomes of democracy when communication is systematically and institutionally stifled and discouraged on the false belief that less communication is best?

VII. What are the limits of communication? We hear again and again that communication is important. But how much can communication accomplish? That is, how much can communication allow us to do? Was the Holocaust a problem of communication? Was slavery a problem of communication? Were Jim Crow laws a problem of communication? Is poverty a problem of communication? Is inequality a problem of communication? In short, can communication solve and resolve all problems?

VIII. Finally, what will the study of communication look like in a world that is increasingly plural and multicultural because of our spaces and distances imploding? How will the rise of this changing world impact communication theory, inquiry, and pedagogy—that is, the theorizing, studying, and teaching of communication? Also, how will the entry of different kinds of people—especially those who have been historically marginalized and disenfranchised in communication studies—impact the studying, theorizing, and teaching of communication?

EPILOGUE

There is a lot of discussion about whether the study of communication (communicology), like biology, psychology, sociology, and anthropology, is a legitimate discipline, or can ever be such (Shepherd, 1993). But why should communicology aspire to be such a discipline?

A discipline represents the organization of a set of ideas in ways that reflect a certain kind of coherence. Any kind of organization involves including certain things and excluding others. Eventually, this process becomes institutionalized, and this is how a discipline emerges. But this is also how a discipline impedes intellectual growth. As a discipline becomes increasingly institutionalized, and thus laying claim to legitimacy, it reinforces and privileges a certain way of studying and understanding something. In doing this, it stifles, undermines, and torments other ways of studying and understanding something. In short, a discipline emerges by cultivating and reinforcing convergence. In this regard, why should communicology aspire to be a discipline? What does the study of communication profit from being hostile to other ways of studying, defining, and understanding communication?

Instead of aspiring to be a discipline and achieving all the institutional trappings that come with a discipline, those who study communication should aspire to be a community of fellow travelers, where the focus should be on nurturing and encouraging all different ways of defining, studying, and understanding communication. Our focus should be on demonstrating how different perspectives add to our knowledge of the human condition. We should aspire to find our integrity and legitimacy in the value and purchase of our contributions to understanding the human experience. This means devising and attending to perspectives of communication that can make valuable contributions. For what is the worth of any discipline that is unable to make valuable contributions to our understanding of the human experience and can only defend its integrity by claiming to be a discipline?

The perspectives found in this book represent only one set of perspectives of communication. There are possibly other perspectives, and even different and better ways of framing and organizing those found in this book. In fact, all disciplines (psychology, anthropology, sociology, etc.) have different perspectives and quarrels between the perspectives. Moreover, all the perspectives found in this book are abstractions, and thus in some ways are distortions of how human beings actually live or study communication. That is, all these perspectives are human creations. We would also do well to remember the words of James W. Carey (2009): "Our models of communication ... create what we disingenuously pretend they merely describe" (p. 15). But again, our focus should always be on showcasing how our perspectives make for valuable contributions to the human experience. Contributions should be our foremost concern. We should be vigilant against becoming disciples of any one perspective. We should always want a diversity of perspectives and the freedom and flexibility to move between different perspectives. We should even want the freedom to be bound to no perspective and even to invent our own perspective.

Yet all perspectives will never be morally and epistemologically equal. Certain perspectives will give us richer insights and understandings than others. Also, some will be much more elegant and heuristic than others. But, in the end, our perspectives are us, meaning that our perspectives can only allow us to perceive and experience what we are willing to perceive and experience. The study of communication will always begin and end with us. Only by pushing against our own emotional, intellectual, existential, and spiritual limits will new perspectives of communication come forth.

CRITICISMS OF LANGUAGE POLITICS

To view communication from the perspective of language and symbols assumes that language inherently has the power to do a variety of things, especially negative and destructive things. Certain kinds of language can harm, offend, and diminish others. As such, certain kinds of language should either be banned or discouraged for the sake of achieving a diverse and inclusive society. This is language politics: removing any language that harms others. However, as well-meaning as this politics is, language has no inherent power to do anything. This forms the foundation of many criticisms of language politics—the struggle over how and what language we should use, and who decides such matters.

The Theoretical Criticism

According to the **Thomas theorem**, a theory in sociology, "If men define situations as real, they are real in their consequences." That is, the interpretation of a situation causes the action and reaction. As such, something is only a problem if you choose to make it a problem. In this case, certain words and symbols are only a problem if you choose to make either a problem. There is no law in the universe that mandates certain words and symbols to be inherently offensive. This is purely our doing. In fact, even the notion of "offensive" is of our making, as many cultures have no such notion. Also, you choosing to make certain words and symbols a problem should in no way obligate the rest of us to do likewise. If anything, human diversity should mean that you should respect my choice just as much as I should respect yours. Indeed, choice theory, a popular theory in psychology, would posit that claiming to find a word or phrase to be offensive is a choice. You have chosen to be angry and feel hurt in response to hearing a word. You have made a choice, and choices have consequences. However, you are by no means devoid of agency and thus purely a victim of language or how another person chooses to use language. You can always make better choices, and should be encouraged to do so. As Don Miguel Ruiz (1997) explains in *The Four Agreements: A Toltec Wisdom Book*, "When you take things personally, then you feel offended, and your reaction is to defend your beliefs and create conflict. You make something big out of something so little, because you have the need to be right and make everybody else wrong. You also try hard to be right by giving them your own opinions. In the same way, whatever you feel and do is just projection of your own personal dream, a reflection of your own agreements. What you say, what you do, and the options you have are according to the agreements you have made—and these opinions have nothing to do with me" (pp. 48–49). Indeed, claiming that certain words, symbols, and phrases make you angry (by triggering you) assumes that your response is natural and even proper. But as Marshall Rosenberg (2015) explains in *Nonviolent Communication: A Language of Life*, when "we are angry, we are finding fault—we are choosing to play God by judging or blaming the other person for being wrong or deserving of punishment" (p. 143). In other words, anger results from us releasing ourselves of being responsible for the condition of our own lives. It represents weakness, as in allowing ourselves to be controlled by our instincts and impulses, and thus being unwilling to look carefully and thoughtfully at the consequences of our actions and decisions.

The Empirical Criticism

Empirical means relying on or derived from observation or experiment. In a comprehensive study of different scholarly literatures in psychology, Scott Lillienfeld (2017), a professor of psychology at Emory University, found negligible support for any of the core assumptions that make microaggression a meaningful psychological construct. Consequently, Lillienfeld calls for an abandoning of the label microaggression and putting a moratorium on microaggression training on college campuses until scholarship emerges that supports the notion. For Lillienfeld, the methodological problem deals with intention, interpretation, and reaction, since what constitutes a microaggression is in the eye of the beholder. Human diversity means that all human beings interpret things differently. What one person may view as a microaggression (e.g., "You speak so eloquently") another can view as a compliment. As Lillienfeld explains, "it is unclear whether any verbal or nonverbal action that a certain proportion of minority individuals perceive as upsetting or offensive would constitute a microaggression. Nor is it apparent what level of agreement among minority group members would be needed to regard a given act as a microaggression. As a consequence, one is left to wonder which actions might fall under the capacious microaggression umbrella" (p. 143). For instance, "Would a discussion of race differences in personality, intelligence, or mental illness in an undergraduate psychology course count? Or a dinner-table conversation regarding the societal pros and cons of affirmative action? What about news coverage of higher crime rates among certain minority populations than among majority populations? It is likely that some of these admittedly uncomfortable topics would elicit pronounced negative emotional reactions among at least some minority group members" (p. 143). In short, the empirical criticism of language politics is that language politics exaggerates the power of language and symbols. No proponent of "hate speech" proscriptions is yet to give any kind of account of how "hate speech" *actually* causes harm. We are merely to assume that because language has power, hateful language has the power to do hateful things. However, if the premise that supports hate speech proscriptions is true, then any person who listens to Hitler—even endlessly—should become a defender of the Holocaust. Evidently, language has no such power. We give language power, or, as choice theory would posit, choose to give language power.

The Pedagogical Criticism

Learning involves challenging everything we value, believe, and fear, thereby disrupting how we perceive, experience, and make sense of things. Simply put, learning succeeds by being violent, by pushing us to do things that are difficult, uncomfortable, and even disturbing. That learning involves challenging what we believe and value means that learning involves challenging our notions of decency and civility. Language politics impedes learning by insidiously undermining the honesty, intensity, and ferocity that is necessary to disrupt our notions of decency and civility. Indeed, to demand, either explicitly or implicitly, that class discussions and readings conform to a certain sensibility is to miss the fact that learning is obligated to disrupt everything, especially what we hold to be sacred. Nothing can be off limits in learning, and invoking race, gender, disability, religion, or sexual orientation to make believe otherwise only stops learning from succeeding. As Henry Giroux, professor of English and cultural studies at McMaster University, notes, "Creating safe spaces runs counter to the notion that learning should be unsettling, that students should challenge common sense assumptions and be willing to confront disturbing realities despite discomfort" (Evans & Giroux, 2016). Indeed, "confronting the intolerable should be challenging and upsetting." It should be "the conditions that produce violence that should upset us ethically and prompt us to act responsibly, rather than to capitulate to a privatized emotional response that substitutes a therapeutic language for a political and worldly one." For Wendy Brown, professor of political science at the University of California, Berkeley, "the domain of free public speech is not one of emotional safety or reassurance" and is "not what the public sphere and political speech promise." Instead, a university education should "call you to think, question, doubt" and "incite you to question everything you assume, think you know or care about" (quoted in Evans & Giroux, 2016).

Similarly, Van Jones believes that the rise of language politics on college campuses in the United States undermines a rigorous liberal democracy. Speaking at the University of Chicago, Jones said that the notion held by students that "I need to be safe ideologically, I need to be safe emotionally, I just need to feel good all the time. And if someone else says something that I don't like that is a problem for everyone else, including the administration," is a "terrible idea" because it undermines the mission of a university education (quoted in Rose, 2017). "I don't want you to be safe ideologically. I don't want you to be safe emotionally. I want you to be strong. That's different. I'm not going to pave the jungle for you. Put on some boots and learn how to deal with adversity. I'm not going to take the weights out of the gym. That's the whole point of the gym. This is the gym [university]. You can't live on a campus where people say stuff that you don't like? ... You are creating a kind of liberalism that the minute it crosses the street into the real world is not just useless, but obnoxious and dangerous. I want you to be offended every single day on this campus. I want you to be deeply aggrieved and offended and upset, and then to learn how to speak back. Because that is what we need from you." In sum, a college education should be profoundly unsettling, beyond the bounds of what any person or group considers civil and decent. After all, as Simon Critchley (2010), Hans Jonas Professor of Philosophy at the New School for Social Research in New York, observes, "Nothing is more common in the history of philosophy than the accusation of impiety."

The Institutional Criticism

Language politics erases and undermines human diversity by demanding institutional solutions to language issues and conflicts. In other words, language politics demands that institutions create and enforce rules and regulations that either stop or undercut different peoples (of different origins and backgrounds) from dealing differently with different language issues and conflicts. In this regard, rather than being on the side of diversity, language politics emerges on the side of conformity and homogeneity. Moreover, in demanding institutional solutions to language issues and conflicts, language politics moves language issues and conflicts from the individual realm to the institutional realm, in the process undermining individual agency and autonomy. That is, besides undermining diversity, language politics, in relying on institutional solutions, undercuts individual initiative and responsibility. As Neil Postman (1979) explains, "Once an institution takes on a problem, to some extent individuals are released from the obligation to solve it themselves. It is true enough that much of the pain and inconvenience of modern life are systemic in their origin and cannot be eliminated without social or political action.... But it is not true that every difficulty, every inadequacy, every failing is entirely social in origin and beyond the range of personal control. Although the liberal point of view does not easily admit it, each person has the capability to take responsibility for some part of his or her life, and of altering that which is painful or destructive" (p. 118). In fact, exercising this capability and taking on this kind of responsibility are vital for human flourishing.

The Contextual Criticism

Language politics is of a worldview that assumes that language is the foundation of communication. As such, words matter, and knowing how to use words properly and correctly is supposedly important. Presumably, our failure to use language properly and correctly is why communication problems arise. But then there is that persistent problem of context, as in "Yes, I know what I said, but you are taking my words out of context." Such an admission reveals that context shapes what words mean. In short, words mean nothing outside of context. As regards communication, contexts exceed words in terms of what is truly important. Without contexts, words meaning nothing, and what words mean is guided and shaped by contexts. So whereas language politics claims that language is important, reality reveals that context is what is *really* important in communication. Consequently, no word is inherently racist or sexist. What words mean must always be understood within a context. Yet knowing what context is shaping the meaning of any word (or set of words) is all but impossible to know reliably as there are many forces (e.g., racial, cultural, historical, political) that shape the context that shape and guide the meaning of words. Thus, any politics that begins on the premise that certain words are inherently offensive reflects no rigorous understanding of communication theory.

The Conceptual Criticism

We commonly assume that sharing a common language is necessary for communication. English-only proponents nearly always point to the Biblical story of Babel to highlight the threat of language diversity. However, lack of a common language has never stopped people from achieving mutual understanding. In fact, the abomination found in the story of Babel came from people speaking a common language—"Now the whole world had one language and common speech." However, "If as one people speaking the same language they have begun to do this [worshipping themselves rather God], then nothing they plan to do will be impossible for them" (Genesis 11). Also, as regards the fear that without a common language a society will descend into chaos and disunity, there is no moment or case study in history that legitimizes this fear. Sharing of a common language did nothing to stop slavery and the Holocaust. In short, language diversity poses no threat to communication. Just like race, gender, ethnicity, sexual orientation, and any other kind of difference, language diversity is only a problem when we choose to make it a problem.

The Legal Criticism

There is a legal position, found in Mari Matsuda, Charles Lawrence, Richard Delgado, and Kimberlé Williams Crenshaw's (1993) *Words that Wound: Critical Race Theory, Assaultive Speech, and the First Amendment* and Jeremy Waldron's (2012) *The Harm in Hate Speech*, that claims free speech needs to be seen within a political and historical context that unevenly and unfairly privileges certain voices that, in too many cases, aim to degrade and undermine the views, positions, and experiences of people who have been historically marginalized. In this case, according to this position, free speech simply means giving these privileged voices the wherewithal to continue to abuse and victimize minority peoples. This position assumes that words have the power to hurt, and thus allowing language to be fully unbridled leaves minority peoples vulnerable to all kinds of abuse under the pretext of free speech. Consequently, the only way to end this situation, according to this view, is to put strict limits on any language that causes harm to minority peoples. However, the problem with this argument is that no context is ever even and fair to all groups. Certain perspectives and experiences will always be privileged and encouraged. Moreover, limiting the public expression of certain kinds of speech does nothing to end the motives and reasons that are giving rise to speech that is being judged as "hateful" and "offensive." Also, who gets to decide what speech should be legally impermissible, and who has the authority to speak on behalf of different minority peoples? In other words, how does any democratic and pluralistic society evenly and fairly decide and adjudicate what speech is legally impermissible? As David Cole (2017) observes in an essay titled "Why We Must Still Defend Free Speech," "It is easy to recognize inequality; it is virtually impossible to articulate a standard for suppression of speech that would not afford government officials dangerously broad discretion and invite discrimination against particular views." Also, why should minority groups "trust representatives of the majority to decide what speech should be censored"? After all, in most cases, which history evidences, the interests of minority groups have always been in conflict with those of the majority. In fact, hate speech codes were originally used to suppress the speech of minority peoples on college campuses under the claim by white students that black students were engaging in racist speech and inviting speakers on campuses who were allegedly guilty of fomenting riots (Lepore, 2017b).

The Ideological Criticism

Language politics undermines human diversity by forcing all of us to use the same language and symbols, and to do so similarly. However, what becomes of diversity when I must find offensive what you find offensive? Why must my sensibility conform to your sensibility? How did your sensibility come to be the sensibility of power and privilege? Moreover, speech codes lessen the intensity and ferocity of language, making only for the illusion of social, racial, and political progress. In other words, these coercive language campaigns only succeed in driving various issues underground rather than pushing us to deal with them openly and honestly. We thereby never develop the temperament that is vital to navigate difficult and even wrenching discussions. As Jill Lepore (2017b), professor of history at Harvard University, reminds us, "All speech is not equal. Some things are true; some things are not. Figuring out how to tell the difference is the work of the university, which rests on a commitment to freedom of inquiry, an unflinching search for truth, and the fearless unmasking of error." Free speech is thus "a long and strenuous argument, as maddening as the past and as painful as the truth."

The Racial/Cultural Criticism

Race and culture figure prominently in what words and phrases we judge to be offensive and derogatory. Whereas people of a certain racial or cultural group may view certain words to be offensive and derogatory, other members of the same group can view the same words and phrases differently. Many examples abound of this reality. It reminds us of the notions of *polysemy*, *polyphony*, and *heteroglossia*—different people sharing the same language but living differently in the language and also using the language to achieve different things. Language is always raced, cultured, and gendered. This reality of different words meaning different things to different people also reminds us that human diversity should always figure prominently in our understanding of things. No word or phrase is inherently offensive or derogatory to all members of any racial or cultural group. It is always a matter of *whom*, as in *who* is judging certain words and phrases to be offensive and derogatory, and *who* gets to dictate or impose such a reality on others? As Mikhail Bakhtin (1986) reminds us, "The words of a language belong to nobody" (p. 88). Finally, divergent communication styles reflect racial and cultural differences. Various peoples simply have no problem with communication practices that others view as offensive and insensitive. For example, in Israel there is the notion of *dugri*, which means truthfulness to the facts or one's opinion, regardless of the impact of the facts or opinions on others. In the Caribbean there is also tremendous value in speaking one's mind, even when doing so publicly could create a lot of commotion ("Mary has no cover for her mouth").

The Historical Criticism

There is no moment in history that shows language politics being responsible for changing the course of history. The ending of slavery, Jim Crow, apartheid in South Africa, the Holocaust, or any other kind of atrocity had nothing to do with language politics. Instead, these horrors came to an end through struggle, sacrifice, and solidarity. Further, there is no evidence that language politics is actually bringing about social and political change. Instead, the threat of sanction, humiliation, and retribution for using "offensive" language only seems to be making for a false civility and collegiality. That a person is now disallowed from publicly saying certain things does nothing to change what the person honestly feels and still says behind closed doors. In other words, language politics is suppressing the kind of honest and difficult communication that comes with dealing with and getting past many wrenching social, racial, and political issues that come with a world where our spaces and distances are increasingly collapsing and imploding.

The Existential Criticism

To profess to be outraged and offended by certain words and symbols is to demand that what you find to be offensive and hurtful should matter equally to the rest of world. But you are merely one among many billions of human beings on this planet. What about all the many things that the rest of us on this planet find to be hurtful and offensive? Where is your outrage over the things that outrage us? Why should what you find to be offensive and hurtful be assumed to be more important than what the rest of the world finds to be so? In fact, why should the rest of the world even care about what you find to be offensive and hurtful, especially when it does nothing to relieve the misery and suffering that others are dealing with? That is, what is the relation between language politics and ending world hunger or helping hundreds of millions of human beings gain access to clean water? How did you come to believe that you are so special, and why should the rest of the world encourage your egotism and narcissism?

The Scriptural Criticism

To claim that language has the power to harm and hurt you is to give language the power of a god. However, the Bible consistently warns against the worshipping of false gods. This is idolatry. There is supposedly only one, true God. ("You shall have no other gods before me." Exodus 20:3; "For where your treasure is, there your heart will be also." Matthew 6:21; "Therefore, my beloved, flee from idolatry." 1 Corinthians 10:14; "In vain do they worship me, teaching as doctrines the commandments of men." Mark 7:7; "Everything that I command you, you shall be careful to do. You shall not add to it or take from it." Deuteronomy 12:32; "Can man make for himself gods? Such are not gods!" Jeremiah 16:20.) Only God has the power to do anything to us, including hurt and harm us. ("Do not be afraid of those who will kill the body but cannot kill the soul. Instead, fear the one who is able to kill both body and soul in hell." Matthew 10:28.) Whereas other human beings certainly have the power to physically hurt and harm us, only God supposedly has the power to truly hurt and harm us. Thus, there is never any need to fear what other human beings can do to us. We should only fear what God can do to us, and because God is supposedly a God of love and mercy, God will never hurt or harm us.

The Spiritual Criticism

In Buddhism, the First Noble Truth is that "There is suffering." To live is to suffer. The challenge is to avoid as much unnecessary suffering as possible and deal constructively with any that remains. However, nearly all of our suffering is of our own making. As Yongey Mingyur Rinpoche (2009), a prominent Tibetan Buddhist master, notes in *Joyful Wisdom: Embracing Change and Finding Freedom*, "Our normal tendency is to assign the cause of suffering to circumstances or conditions ... however, the cause of suffering lies not events or circumstances, but in the way we perceive and interpret our experiences as it unfolds" (pp. 63–64). We make our own suffering by viewing ourselves at the center of everything and thereby demanding that everything conforms to our wants, desires, aspirations, needs, and expectations. However, to avoid suffering, removing ourselves from our perspectives is necessary. In other words, removing our narcissism becomes an important spiritual exercise. We must develop a perspective of things that in no way begins with us being at the center of everything. What certain words and phrases mean to us is nothing but a creature of our own perspective of things. The same words and phrases can mean completely different things from different perspectives. Thus what matters in the end is our *perspective* of things rather than our *meaning* of things. For as the Buddha teaches, "When the mind exists undisturbed in the Way, nothing in the world can offend, and when a thing can no longer offend, it ceases to exist in the old way" (Kononenko & Kononenko, 2010, p. 146).

The Epistemological Criticism

Language politics assumes that meaning resides in words and symbols. Banishing and banning words and symbols are supposedly necessary to stop various meanings from circulating and causing harm, especially to people who have been historically brutalized and marginalized. We are to assume that certain words and symbols are inherently "hateful" and "harmful" and that such words and symbols incite hate and cause harm. However, meaning resides within us rather than in words or symbols. As Lee Thayer (2011) reminds us, "Words do not contain or convey meaning. To the contrary, humans impose meanings on words" (p. 104). That the US Constitution or any set of religious scriptures lends for different and conflicting interpretations validates this point. Any fostering of a fear of language through threat of sanction and retribution impedes the rise of new meanings and interpretations and, consequently, the rise of new ways of perceiving and understanding things. Indeed, nearly every prophet was accused and persecuted for saying things that were generally assumed and judged to be offensive. In this way, language politics, though born of good intentions, puts us on the wrong side of history.

GLOSSARY

attribution   Attaching motives to the actions and decisions of others.

attunement   Promotes harmony between human beings by allowing us to feel and know what others are feeling and knowing.

biases of power   The idea that power changes our perception and understanding of things.

carnivalization   The tension between diverging and homogenizing forces found in language.

centrifugal   Forces that impede and undermine ways of speaking and writing that aim to unite people around a common worldview by standardizing and homogenizing our speaking and writing practices.

centripetal   Forces that create and promote norms of speaking and writing that aim to unite people around a common worldview by standardizing and homogenizing our speaking and writing practices.

choice theory   A theory positing that the choices we make are central to our existence.

chronemics   Nonverbal messages that deal with time.

cognitive biases   Our tendency to respond favorably to scenarios that are framed positively rather than negatively.

cognitive complexity   Our tolerance for ambiguity and confusion.

coherence (narrative)   The degree to which a story makes sense.

confirmation bias   Our tendency to focus favorably on facts, opinions, and findings that support our pre-existing views of something, and to dismiss those facts, opinions, and findings that do the opposite.

confusion   Lacking clarity and precision in our description of events and things.

constitutive (language)   Language is full of rules, and these rules become our rules, or the rules that will define us and shape how we engage with the world and each other.

construction of biased social theory   Our tendency to develop explanations of things that conform to our own values, beliefs, and fears, which means we subconsciously neglect, exclude, and downplay facts, opinions, and findings that do not conform.

context collapse   The proper context necessary to understand something correctly being lost as a result of changing conditions that an encoder has no control over.

convergence theory   A theory positing that as communication increases, variation within systems decreases.

cyborgs   A person whose limits have been extended beyond their natural limits by physically incorporating mechanical elements in the body.

deception   Distorting, twisting, and manipulating our reality for personal gain.

deplatforming   A new form of activism that is about refusing to allow individuals with certain views to have a stage and thus an audience.

derogation of others   Our tendency to derogate others when we feel threatened.

descriptive language   Describing things in ways that reflect no personal biases or prejudices.

dialect   Any language that lacks political power and privilege.

dialogic stance   Always being open to the possibility of something new—as in a new interpretation, a new revelation, a new meaning, a new understanding—emerging out of the world's boundless ambiguity.

disqualification   Insisting and asserting that only people with certain expertise and experience can speak.

divergent thinking   Thinking about things in ways that disrupt the order of things that make new and better things possible.

dugri   A notion found in the Hebrew language that refers to speaking honestly and courageously, regardless of the consequences.

emotional contagion   Our emotions and behaviors directly shaping the emotions and behaviors of others in similar ways.

ethics   The systems that guide what actions and behaviors we judge to be right or wrong.

evaluative language   Descriptions that reflect personal biases and prejudices.

extended mind hypothesis   The idea that the resources and conditions found in our environments impact the workings of our minds.

false personal narratives   Our tendency to unfairly blame others for our own failings and shortcomings.

feng shui   A philosophy that teaches how to harmonize the energy in an environment to assure good fortune for those inhabiting that space and place.

fidelity (narrative)   The truthfulness or reliability of a story.

framing effects   Organizing and positioning words in ways that appeal to our cognitive biases to achieve various outcomes.

futurists   People who believe technology represents the next stage in human evolution, and thus will make for superior quality of life.

generosity   Giving others the benefit of the doubt.

haptics   Nonverbal communication that deals with touch.

hegemony   A dominant set of conceptual and material arrangements that shape how we perceive, experience, and make sense of things.

heteroglossia   Using the same language to accomplish different goals and objectives.

homophony   Differently spelled words sounding alike.

humility   Recognizing the limits of our ability to understand things and people perfectly and correctly.

ideograph   Concepts that cultivate, reinforce, and weaponize an ideology.

ideological view   A perspective of language that focuses on how language cultivates and propagates various beliefs, fears, values, and ambitions.

ideology   A common system of beliefs, values, fears, ambitions, and norms that we accept as true.

illusion of control   Our tendency to believe that we have greater control in shaping the outcomes of things than we actually do.

impression   Arriving at an understanding of someone or something based on scant information.

impression management theory   A theory that claims communication is fundamentally about us managing the impressions that others form of us.

information theory   A theory that helps explain why groups that share more information achieve more convergence, and those that share less have more divergence.

in-group/out-group associations   Our tendency to view favorably those we perceive as being like us, and to view unfavorably those we perceive as being different to us.

I-It   Any action or decision that diminishes the humanity of others.

intrapersonal communication   Any communication that happens inside of us.

I-Thou   Recognizing our own humanity in the humanity of others.

kinesics   Nonverbal communication that reflects body language.

kus dili   A term for whistling languages found in Turkey.

language politics   The struggle over who controls how we use language and what language should define and guide a society.

legitimation   Rationalizing and justifying decisions and practices by invoking higher order explanatory devices.

magical view   A perspective of language that focuses on the power of language to reveal new truths, new meanings, and new experiences.

master narratives   Narratives that validate and cultivate the ideological and material interests of elites.

maunam   A concept found in Hinduism that refers to achieving a new state of being by deliberately restraining from speech.

media ecology   A perspective in communication studies that assumes that in order to understand things—such as any technology—we have to understand the environments that make, situate, and legitimize those things.

microaggressions   Everyday verbal, nonverbal, and environmental slights, snubs, or insults, whether intentional or unintentional, directed to any person of a historically marginalized group.

monologic stance   Aims to cultivate and institutionalize one truth, one meaning, or one understanding by removing ambiguity and suppressing conflict.

narcissism   Being obsessed with our own reality and humanity, thereby making empathy impossible.

naturalization   Treating something that is produced by human beings as natural and belonging to the world.

neuroplasticity   The ability of the brain to change continuously throughout a person's life.

neutralization   Assuming that communication is devoid of values.

nommo   A concept found in Africa claiming that through the spoken word human beings have the power to actualize life and attain mastery over things.

oculesics   Nonverbal communication that refers to patterns of fixation.

open systems   Any system that is permeable and vulnerable to new meanings and interpretations.

originalism   A legal philosophy that views the (United States) Constitution's meaning as fixed at the time of enactment.

pacification   The process by which conflict or dissent is suppressed through an apparently reasonable attempt to engage in it.

paralinguistics   Nonverbal communication that deals with voice inflections.

perception   Selecting, organizing, and interpreting a message in ways that conform to our understanding of things.

physical noise   Physical and material things in our environments that make it difficult to decode or listen to the meaning of a message.

physiological noise   Distraction caused by hunger, fatigue, headaches, medication, and other factors that affect how we feel and think.

plausible deniability   Strategically using ambiguity to avoid clarity of intention and motivation.

politics   The things we struggle over and the means we use to do so.

polyphony   Different groups using the same language differently; for example, different races and different social classes using the same language differently.

polysemy   Words have many different meanings.

proxemics   Nonverbal communication that reflects space and distance.

psychological noise   Refers to qualities in us (like our biases) that affect how we communicate with and interpret others.

recursivity   Our treatment of others shapes us accordingly.

reflective (language)   Human beings use language—like a tool—to perform various tasks and functions, such as creating and sustaining various discourses about different things.

representational view   A perspective of language that focuses on using language precisely and correctly.

right speech   A concept found in Buddhism that reflects a set of desirable and positive communication practices.

role theory   A theory that claims human beings are always adopting and embodying different roles and performances.

Sapir-Whorf hypothesis   Different languages reflect different minds, and different minds reflect different worldviews.

self-inflation   Our tendency to highlight our accomplishments and downplay our failures, as well as our tendency to spotlight our desirable features and attributes and to mask those that are less so.

semantic noise   Ambiguity in language resulting in confusion and distortion.

shantam   A concept found in Hinduism that connotes peace and bliss.

singularity   The final merging of machines and human beings.

situational thinking   Dealing with reality on its own terms and conditions.

social brain hypothesis   A theory that claims the evolutionary need for communication systems to manage the demands and tensions of complex social relationships is responsible for the superior size of our brains and also the increasing capacity of our brains.

social capital   The quality and quantity of relationships found in a community.

social desirability bias   The unwillingness of respondents to share embarrassing information with others, including researchers.

sound effect words   Words that resemble or imitate the source of the sound they describe.

space-biased media   Any social technology, like radio and television, that conveys information to large numbers of people but has short exposure times.

strange attractor   A self-organizing force found in all living systems.

subjectification of experience   Invoking one's opinion to stop any further discussion.

Thomas theorem   A theory positing that the interpretation of a situation causes the action and reaction.

time-biased media   Any social technology, like manuscripts and engravings on temple walls, that conveys information to a small number of people but has long exposure times.

toguna   A meeting house normally located in the center of a Dogon village.

topic avoidance   Suppressing the open expression of conflict and dissent by prohibiting or discouraging the discussion of some events and feelings.

transactional process   A model of communication that assumes communication emerges by reducing or removing confusion.

transpersonal communication   Assumes a realm of communication beyond our five physical senses, as in two people communicating without using any of these senses.

transubstantiation   The act of transforming the culture of another group into one's own culture and, consequently, converting the symbols and behaviors of others into those consistent with one's own epistemology, or system of knowing and understanding the world.

ubuntu   An African relational concept referring to one person becoming human through other human beings.

uncertainty reduction theory   A theory that assumes people strive to reduce the uncertainty of others by seeking information about them.

Universal Grammar   A theory that assumes languages inherently share the same underlying structures, and thus all possess the same capacity to convey complex thoughts.

verbal-ideological world   Forces that aim to make our manner of speaking and writing consistent with dominant values, beliefs, and fears.

vulnerability   Our willingness to suspend everything we believe and value.

REFERENCES

Adler, R. B., Rodman, G., & du Pré, A. (2017). *Understanding human communication*. New York, NY: Oxford University Press.

Alberts, J. K., Nakayama, T. K., & Martin, J. N. (2007). *Human communication in society*. Upper Saddle River, NJ: Pearson Prentice Hall.

Alter, A. (2017). *Irresistible: The rise of addictive technology and the business of keeping us hooked*. New York, NY: Penguin Books.

Anton, C. (2007). On the nonlinearity of human communication: Insatiability, context, form. *Atlantic Journal of Communication*, *15*(2), 79–102. https://doi.org/10.1080/15456870701215834

Axelrod, R. (1984). *The evolution of cooperation*. New York, NY: Basic Books.

Bakhtin, M. M. (1986). *Speech genres and other late essays*. Austin, TX: University of Texas Press.

Bakhtin, M. M. (2008). *The dialogic imagination: Four essays*. Austin, TX: University of Texas Press.

Bateson, G. (2000). *Steps of an ecology of mind*. Chicago, IL: University of Chicago Press.

Beilock, S. (2015). *How the mind knows its body*. New York, NY: Atria Books.

Bickerton, D. (1995). *Language and human behavior.* Seattle, WA: University of Washington Press.

Blake, A. (2017, February 1). Neil Gorsuch, Antonin Scalia and originalism, explained. *Washington Post*. Retrieved from https://www.washingtonpost.com/news/the-fix/wp/2017/02/01/neil-gorsuch-antonin-scalia-and-originalism-explained/

Bohaker, H. (2014). Indigenous histories and archival media in the early modern Great Lakes. In M. Cohen & J. Glover (Eds.), *Colonial mediascapes: Sensory worlds of the early Americas* (pp. 99–140). Lincoln, NB: University of Nebraska Press.

Bohm, D. (1985). *Unfolding meaning*. New York, NY: Routledge.

Bork, R. (2005). *A country I do not recognize: The legal assault on American values*. Stanford, CA: Hoover Institution Press.

Brady, T. P. (1954). *Black Monday: Segregation or amalgamation*. Winona, MS: Association of Citizens' Councils.

Brewer, E., & Westerman, J. (2017). *Organizational communication: Today's professional life in context*. New York, NY: Oxford University Press.

Brody, J. E. (2017, June 12). Social interaction is critical for mental and physical health. *New York Times*. Retrieved from https://www.nytimes.com/2017/06/12/well/live/having-friends-is-good-for-you.html?module=inline

Brokaw, G. (2014). Semiotics, aesthetics, and the *Quechua* concept of *Quilca*. In M. Cohen & J. Glover (Eds.), *Colonial mediascapes: Sensory worlds of the early Americas* (pp. 166–202). Lincoln, NB: University of Nebraska Press.

Buber, M. (2013). *I and thou*. New York, NY: Bloomsbury.

Burke, K. (1989). *On symbols and society*. Chicago, IL: University of Chicago Press.

Burleson, B. (1997). A different voice on different cultures: Illusion and reality in the study of sex differences in personal relationships. *Personal Relationships*, 4(3), 229–41. https://doi.org/10.1111/j.1475-6811.1997.tb00142.x

Campbell, A. F. (2019, July 3). California is about to ban discrimination against black workers with natural hairstyles. *Vox*. Retrieved from https://www.vox.com/identities/2019/7/3/20680946/california-crown-act-natural-hair-discrimination

Carey, J. W. (2009). A cultural approach to communication. In J. W. Carey (Ed.), *Communication as culture: Essays on media and society* (rev. ed., pp. 1–17). New York, NY: Routledge.

Carlson, F. (2015, January 23). Say what? Half of the world's language will vanish by the end of the century. *PBS News Hour*. Retrieved from https://www.pbs.org/newshour/arts/new-documentary-explores-languages-peril-around-globe

Carroll, C. E. (2013). *The handbook of communication and corporate reputation*. Malden, MA: John Wiley & Sons.

Chamberlin, J. E. (2003). *If this is your land, where are your stories?* Cleveland, OH: Pilgrim Press.

Chesebro, J. W., & Bertelsen, D. A. (1996). *Analyzing media: Communication technologies as symbolic and cognitive systems*. New York, NY: Guilford Press.

Chomsky, N. (2006). *Language and mind*. New York, NY: Cambridge University Press.

Clark, A. (2003). *Natural-born cyborgs: Minds, technologies, and the future of human intelligence*. New York, NY: Oxford University Press.

Cole, D. (2017, September 28). Why we must still defend free speech. *New York Review of Books*. Retrieved from https://www.nybooks.com/articles/2017/09/28/why-we-must-still-defend-free-speech/

Colt, G. H. (1997, August). The magic of touch. *Life*. Retrieved from http://t4.stthom.edu/users/smith/christmorallife/touch.pdf

Condit, C. M. (2006). Communication as relationality. In G. J. Shepherd, J. St. John, & T. Striphas (Eds.), *Communication as ... Perspectives on theory* (pp. 3–12). Thousand Oaks, CA: Sage.

Conquergood, D. (2002). Performance studies: Interventions and radical research. *Drama Review*, 46(2), 145–56. https://doi.org/10.1162/105420402320980550

Cortazzi, M. (2001). Narrative analysis in ethnography. In P. Atkinson, A. Coffey, S. Delamont, L. Lofland, & J. Lofland (Eds.), *Handbook of ethnography* (pp. 384–94). London, UK: Sage.

Crawford, F. (2006, July 25). The sound of a word tells us something about how it is used, Cornell study finds. *Cornell Chronicle*. Retrieved from https://news.cornell.edu/stories/2006/07/cu-study-finds-connection-between-sound-and-meaning-words

Crawford, L. (1996). Everyday Tao: Conversation and contemplation. *Communication Studies, 47*(1–2), 25–34. https://doi.org/10.1080/10510979609368461

Critchley, S. (2010, May 16). What is a philosopher? *New York Times*. Retrieved from https://opinionator.blogs.nytimes.com/2010/05/16/what-is-a-philosopher/

Cronen, V. E. (1998). Communication theory for the twenty-first century: Cleaning up the wreckage of the psychology project. In J. S. Trent (Ed.), *Communication views from the helm for the 21st century* (pp. 18–38). Needham Heights, MA: Allyn and Bacon.

Cunningham-Parmeter, K. (2012). Alien language: Immigration metaphors and the jurisprudence of otherness. *Fordham Law Review, 79*, 1545–98. https://ssrn.com/abstract=1803473

Dainton, M., & Zelley, E. D. (2018). *Applying communication theory for professional life.* Thousand Oaks, CA: Sage.

Darwin, C. (1871). *Descent of man*. London, UK: John Murray.

Davis, D. K., & Jasinski, J. (1993). Beyond the culture wars: An agenda for research on communication and culture. *Journal of Communication, 43*(3), 141–49. https://doi.org/10.1111/j.1460-2466.1993.tb01286.x

de Looze, L. (2016). *The letter and the cosmos: How the alphabet has shaped the western view of the world*. Toronto, ON: University of Toronto Press.

Deetz, S. (1992). *Democracy in an age of corporate colonization: Developments in communication and the politics of everyday life.* New York, NY: SUNY Press.

Denard, C. C. (2008). A bench by the road: *Beloved* by Toni Morrison. In C. C. Denard (Eds.), *Toni Morrison: Conversations* (pp. 44–50). Jackson, MS: University Press of Mississippi.

Dennett, D. C. (1994). The role of language in intelligence. In Jean Khalfa (Ed.), *What is intelligence? The Darwin College lectures* (pp. 161–78). Cambridge, UK: Cambridge University Press.

Derrida, J. (1977). *Signature, event, context*. Evanston, IL: Northwestern University Press.

DeVito, J. (1993). *Messages: Building interpersonal communication skills.* New York, NY: HarperCollins.

Dostie, R. L. (2019, June 22). She didn't act like a rape victim. *New York Times*. Retrieved from https://www.nytimes.com/2019/07/22/opinion/armed-forces-rape.html?action=click&module=Opinion&pgtype=Homepage&login=email&auth=login-email

Duck, S., & McMahan, D. T. (2017). *Communication in everyday life.* Thousand Oaks, CA: Sage.

Dunbar, R. (2002). The social brain hypothesis. In J. T. Cacioppo, G. G. Berntson, R. Adolphs, C. S. Carter, M. K. McClintock, M. J. Meaney, ... & S. E. Taylor (Eds.), *Foundations in social neuroscience* (pp. 69–88). Cambridge, MA: MIT Press.

Dynarski, S. M. (2017, August 10). For better learning in college lectures, lay down the laptop and pick up a pen. *Brookings*. Retrieved from https://www.brookings.edu/research/for-better-learning-in-college-lectures-lay-down-the-laptop-and-pick-up-a-pen/amp/

Eades, J. (2019, February 13). When the best leaders use coaching vs feedback. *Learn Loft*. Retrieved from https://learnloftblog.com/2019/02/13/when-the-best-leaders-use-coaching-vs-feedback/

Engen, D. E. (2002). The communicative imagination and its cultivation. *Communication Quarterly, 50*(1), 41–57. https://doi.org/10.1080/01463370209385645

Evans, B., & Giroux, H. (2016, June 20). The violence of forgetting. *New York Times*. Retrieved from https://www.nytimes.com/2016/06/20/opinion/the-violence-of-forgetting.html

Eze, M. O. (2010). *Intellectual history in contemporary South Africa*. New York, NY: Palgrave Macmillan.

Fanon, F. (2008). *Black skin, white masks*. New York, NY: Grove Press.

Fassett, D. L., Warren, J. T., & Nainby, K. (2018). *Communication: A critical/cultural introduction*. San Diego, CA: Cognella.

Fezehai, M. (2019, May 30). In Turkey, keeping a language of whistles alive. *New York Times*. Retrieved from https://www.nytimes.com/2019/05/30/arts/in-turkey-keeping-alive-a-language-of-whistles.html?action=click&module=Editors%20Picks&pgtype=Homepage

Fisher, W. R. (1987). *Human communication as narration: Toward a philosophy of reason, value, and action*. Columbia, SC: University of South Carolina Press.

Frankl, V. (2006). *Man's search for meaning*. Boston, MA: Beacon Press.

Fukuyama, F. (2011). *The origins of political order*. New York, NY: Farrar, Straus and Giroux.

Gearhart, S. M. (1979). The womanization of rhetoric. *Women's Studies International Quarterly, 2*, 195–201. https://doi.org/10.1016/s0148-0685(79)91809-8

Gerbner, G. (1974). Communication: Society is the message. *Communication, 1*, 57–64.

Gergen, K. (2009). *Relational being: Beyond self and community*. New York, NY: Oxford University Press.

Ginsburg, K. R. (2007). The importance of play in promoting healthy child development and maintaining strong parent–child bonds. *Pediatrics, 119*(1), 182–91 https://doi.org/10.1542/peds.2006-2697

Goffman, E. (1959). *The presentation of self in everyday life*. New York, NY: Doubleday.

Goldsmith, D. J., & Fulfs, P. A. (1999). "You just don't have the evidence": An analysis of claims and evidence in Deborah Tannen's *You Just Don't Understand*. In M. E. Roloff (Ed.), *Communication Yearbook 22* (pp. 1–49). Thousand Oaks, CA: Sage.

Gopnik, A. (2016, May 9). Feel me: What the new science of touch says about ourselves. *New Yorker*. Retrieved from https://www.newyorker.com/magazine/2016/05/16/what-the-science-of-touch-says-about-us

Greenspan, S. I., & Shanker, S. G. (2004). *The first idea: How symbols, language, and intelligence evolved from our primate ancestors to modern humans*. Cambridge, MA: Da Capo Press.

Griffin, E., Ledbetter, A., & Sparks, G. (2015). *A first look at communication theory*. New York, NY: McGraw Hill.

Hamlet, J. D. (2011, Spring). Word! The African American oral tradition and its rhetorical impact on American popular culture. *Black History Bulletin*. Retrieved from https://www.questia.com/read/1G1-273615269/word-the-african-american-oral-tradition-and-its

Hanh, T. N. (1991). *Old path white clouds: Walking in the footsteps of the Buddha.* Berkeley, CA: Parallax Press Books.

Hanh, T. N. (2013). *The art of communicating.* New York, NY: HarperCollins.

Harris, M. (2014). *The end of absence: Reclaiming what we've lost in a world of constant connection.* New York, NY: Penguin.

Harris, S. (2010). *The moral landscape: How science can determine human values.* New York, NY: Free Press.

Hedeager, H. (2011). Is language unique to human species? Retrieved from http://www.columbia.edu/~rmk7/HC/HC_Readings/AnimalComm.pdf

Heilman, S. C. (1979). Communication and interaction: A parallel in the theoretical outlooks of Erving Goffman and Ray Birdwhistell. *Communication, 4,* 221–34.

Hinman, L. M. (1982). Nietzsche, metaphor, and truth. *Philosophy and Phenomenological Research, 43*(2), 179–99. https://doi.org/10.2307/2107528

Holland, J. S. (2011). *Unlikely friendships: 47 remarkable stories from the animal kingdom.* New York, NY: Workman Publishing.

Holland, J. S. (2013). *Unlikely loves: 47 heartwarming true stories from the animal kingdom.* New York, NY: Workman Publishing.

Holm, A. (2013, December 10). Linguistics professor explains why sound effects words matter. *The Daily Universe.* Retrieved from https://universe.byu.edu/2013/12/10/linguistics-professor-explains-why-sound-effect-words-matter/

Houseley, W., Nicholls, T., & Southwell, R. (2013). *Managing in the media.* Woburn, MA: Focal Press.

Huntington, S. (1997). *Clash of civilizations and the remaking of world order.* New York, NY: Touchstone.

Huntington, S. (2004). *Who we are: The challenges to America's national identity.* New York, NY: Simon & Schuster.

Innis, H. A. (2007). *Empire and communications.* Toronto, ON: Dundurn Press.

Jain, N. C., & Matukumalli, A. (1994, November). *The functions of silence in India: Implications for intercultural communication research.* Paper presented at the annual convention of the Speech Communication Association, New Orleans, Louisiana.

Jasinski, J. (2001). *Sourcebook on rhetoric: Key concepts in contemporary rhetorical studies.* Thousand Oaks, CA: Sage.

Jasmin, K., & Casasanto, D. (2012). The QWERTY effect: How typing shapes the meanings of words. *Psychonomic Bulletin & Review, 19*(3), 499–504. https://doi.org/10.3758/s13423-012-0229-7

Johnson, M. (2007). *The meaning of the body: Aesthetics of human understanding.* Chicago, IL: University of Chicago Press.

Jones, Jr., R. G. (2017). Communication in the real world. Boston, MA: FlatWorld. Retrieved from https://scholar.flatworldknowledge.com/books/30863/jones_1.0-ch01_s01/preview

Keohane, J. (2010, June 11). How facts backfire. *Boston Globe.* Retrieved from http://archive.boston.com/news/science/articles/2010/07/11/how_facts_backfire/

Khan Academy. (2019). Early civilizations. Retrieved from https://www.khanacademy.org/humanities/world-history/world-history-beginnings/birth-agriculture-neolithic-revolution/a/introduction-what-is-civilization

Khatchadourian, R. (2018, November 19). Degrees of freedom. *New Yorker*. Retrieved from https://www.newyorker.com/magazine/2018/11/26/how-to-control-a-machine-with-your-brain

Konnikova, M. (2014, June 3). What's lost as handwriting fades. *New York Times*. Retrieved from https://www.nytimes.com/2014/06/03/science/whats-lost-as-handwriting-fades.html

Kononenko, I., & Kononenko, I. R. (2010). *Teachers of wisdom*. Pittsburgh, PA: Rose Dog Books.

Kosfeld, M., Heinrichs, M., Zak, P. J., Fischbacher, U., & Fehr, E. (2005). Oxytocin increases trust in humans. *Nature, 435*, 673–76. https://doi.org/10.1038/nature03701

Kumar, A., & Epley, N. (2018). Undervaluing gratitude: Expressers misunderstanding the consequences of showing appreciation. *Psychological Science, 29(9)*, 1423–35. https://doi.org/10.1177/0956797618772506

Ladegaard, H. J. (2017). *The discourse of powerlessness and repression*. New York, NY: Routledge.

Lanier, J. (2010). *You are not a gadget*. New York, NY: Knopf.

Le Beau Lucchesi, E. (2017, June 4). The empathetic dog. *New York Times*. Retrieved from https://www.nytimes.com/2017/06/04/well/family/the-empathetic-dog.html?action=click&pgtype=Homepage&version=Moth-Visible&moduleDetail=inside-nyt-region-2&module=inside-nyt-region&region=inside-nyt-region&WT.nav=inside-nyt-region

Leder, S. (2017). *More beautiful than before: How suffering transforms us*. Carlsbad, CA: Hay House.

Lepore, J. (2017a, March 20). The history test: How should the courts use the Constitution? *New Yorker*. Retrieved from https://www.newyorker.com/magazine/2017/03/27/weaponizing-the-past

Lepore, J. (2017b, October 9). Inquietude (flip-flopping on free speech). *New Yorker*. Retrieved from https://www.newyorker.com/magazine/2017/10/09/flip-flopping-on-free-speech

Levine, D. N. (1985). *The flight from ambiguity: Essays in social and cultural theory*. Chicago, IL: University of Chicago Press.

Levy, K. (2017, March 22). The problems with originalism. *New York Times*. Retrieved from https://www.nytimes.com/2017/03/22/opinion/the-problems-with-originalism.html

Liberman, M. (2012, December 12). Literary moist aversion. Retrieved from http://languagelog.ldc.upenn.edu/nll/?p=4389

Lillienfeld, S. O. (2017). Microaggressions: Strong claims, inadequate evidence. *Perspectives on Psychological Science, 12*(1), 138–69. https://doi.org/10.1177/1745691616659391

Lingis, A. (1994). *The community of those who have nothing in common*. Bloomington, IN: Indiana University Press.

Littlejohn, S. W. (1996). *Theories of human communication* (5th ed.). Belmont, CA: Wadsworth.

Lupher, D. A. (2003). *Romans in the new world*. Ann Arbor, MI: University of Michigan Press.

MacIntyre, A. (2007). *After virtue* (3rd ed.). Notre Dame, IN: University of Notre Dame Press.

Matsuda, M. J., Lawrence, C., Delgado, R., & Crenshaw, K. W. (1993). *Words that wound: Critical race theory, assaultive speech, and the First Amendment*. Boulder, CO: Westview Press.

McGee, M. C. (1980). The "ideograph": The link between rhetoric and ideology. *Quarterly Journal of Speech, 66*, 1–16.

McLuhan, M. (1962). *The Gutenberg galaxy: The making of typographic man.* Toronto, ON: University of Toronto Press.

McNamee, S., & Gergen, K. J. (1999). Relational responsibility: Resources for sustainable dialogue. In S. McNamee & K. J. Gergen (Eds.), *An invitation to relational responsibility* (pp. 3–12). Thousand Oaks, CA: Sage.

Miller, G., & Steinberg, M. (1975). *Between people: A new analysis of interpersonal communication.* Chicago, IL: Science Research Associates.

Mithen, S. (2015, November 19). On ancestor apes in Europe. *New York Review of Books.* Retrieved from https://www.nybooks.com/articles/2015/11/19/ancestor-apes -europe/

Mortensen, C. D. (1991). Communication, conflict, and culture. *Communication Theory, 1*(4), 273–93. https://doi.org/10.1111/j.1468-2885.1991.tb00021.x

National Communication Association (NCA). (2019). Learning outcomes in communication project. Retrieved from https://www.natcom.org/about-nca/what-communication

Nelson, A. (2016, June 24). Gender communication: It's complicated. *Psychology Today.* Retrieved from https://www.psychologytoday.com/us/blog/he-speaks-she-speaks /201606/gender-communication-it-s-complicated

Neuliep, J. W. (2015). *Intercultural communication: A contextual approach.* Thousand Oaks, CA: Sage.

Nussbaum, M. (1997). *Cultivating humanity: A classical defense of reform in liberal education.* Cambridge, MA: Harvard University Press.

Ong, W. (1982). *Literacy and orality.* New York, NY: Taylor & Francis.

Ortiz, S. (2003). Song, poetry and language—Expression and perception. In M. J. Moore (Ed.), *Genocide of the mind: New Native American writing* (pp. 105–18). New York, NY: Nation Books.

Paliszkiewicz, J., & Madra-Sawicka, M. (2016). Impression management in social media: The example of LinkedIn. *Management, 11*, 203–12.

Parvanta, C. F., Nelson, D. E., & Harner, R. N. (2018). *Public health communication: Critical tools and strategies.* Burlington, MA: Jones & Bartlett Learning.

Pearce, W. B. (2012). Evolution and transformation. In C. Creede, B. Fisher-Yoshida, & P. V. Gallegos (Eds.), *The reflective, facilitative and interpretative practices of coordinated management of meaning* (pp. 1–21). Lanham, MD: Rowman & Littlefield.

Perloff, R. M. (2003). *The dynamics of persuasion: Communication and attitudes in the 21st century.* Mahwah, NJ: Lawrence Erlbaum.

Phillips, D. (2019, May 2). This is unacceptable. Military reports a surge of sexual assaults in the ranks. *New York Times.* Retrieved from https://www.nytimes.com /2019/05/02/us/military-sexual-assault.html?action=click&module=RelatedLinks &pgtype=Article

Pinker, S. (1994). *The language instinct: How the mind creates language.* New York, NY: HarperCollins.

Pinsky, R. (2010, August 13). Start the presses. *New York Times Book Review.* Retrieved from https://www.nytimes.com/2010/08/15/books/review/Pinsky-t.html

Postman, N. (1979). *Teaching as a conserving activity.* New York, NY: Dell.

Postman, N. (1993). *Technopoly: The surrender of culture to technology.* New York, NY: Vintage Books.

Ramos, V. J. (2019). *Analyzing the role of cognitive biases in the decision-making process.* Hershey, PA: IGI Global.

Rasmussen, B. B. (2014). The manuscript, the Quipu, and the early American book. In M. Cohen & J. Glover (Eds.), *Colonial mediascapes: Sensory worlds of the early Americas* (pp. 141–65). Lincoln, NB: University of Nebraska Press.

Ratcliffe, S. (Ed.). (2010). *Oxford dictionary of quotations by subject.* New York, NY: Oxford University Press.

Redmond, M. (2015). Symbolic interactionism. *English Technical Reports and White Papers, 4.* Retrieved from https://lib.dr.iastate.edu/cgi/viewcontent.cgi?article=1004&context =engl_reports

Reese, B. (2013). *Infinite progress: How the internet and technology will end ignorance, disease, poverty, hunger, and war.* Austin, TX: Greenleaf Book Group Press.

Reese, B. (2018). *The fourth age: Smart robots, conscious computers, and the future of humanity.* New York, NY: Atria Books.

Richmond, V. P., & McCroskey, J. C. (2009). *Organizational communication for survival: Making work, work.* Boston, MA: Pearson.

Rinpoche, Y. M. (2009). *Joyful wisdom: Embracing change and finding freedom.* New York, NY: Three Rivers Press.

Robinson, A. (2007). *The story of writing: Alphabets, hieroglyphs & pictograms.* London, UK: Thames & Hudson.

Rodriguez, A. (2003). *Diversity as liberation (II): Introducing a new understanding of diversity.* New York, NY: Hampton Press.

Rodriguez, A. (2015). Understanding graffiti: Multidisciplinary studies from prehistory to the present. In T. R. Lovata & E. Olton (Eds.), *On the origins of anonymous texts that appear on walls* (pp. 21–31). Walnut Creek, CA: Left Coast Press.

Rodriguez, A. (2018). *Against inclusion: Tyranny in the name of diversity.* New York, NY: Public Square Press.

Rodriguez, A., & Clair, R. P. (1999). Graffiti as communication: Exploring the discursive tensions of anonymous texts. *Southern Communication Journal, 65*(1), 1–15. https://doi.org/10.1080/10417949909373152

Rose, F. (2017, March 30). Safe spaces on college campuses are creating intolerant students. *Huffington Post.* Retrieved from https://www.cato.org/publications /commentary/safe-spaces-college-campuses-are-creating-intolerant-students

Rosenberg, M. B. (2015). *Nonviolent communication: A language of life.* Encinitas, CA: PuddleDancer Press.

Ruiz, D. M. (1997). *The four agreements: A Toltec wisdom book.* San Rafael, CA: Amber-Allen.

Samovar, L. A., Porter, R. E., McDaniel, E. R., & Roy, C. S. (2015). *Intercultural communication: A reader.* Boston, MA: Cengage Learning.

Sanders, S. R. (1997). The power of stories. *The Georgia Review, 51,* 113–26.

Sanders, S. R. (2000). *The force of spirit.* Boston, MA: Beacon Press.

Sapir, E. (1961). *Culture, language and personality: Selected essays.* Berkeley, CA: University of California Press.

Saracho, O. (2002). Young children's creativity and pretend play. *Early Child Development and Care, 172(5)*, 431–38. https://doi.org/10.1080/03004430214553

Saral, T. B. (1983). Hindu philosophy of communication. *Communication, 8*, 47–58.

Schmidt, A. J. (1997). *The menace of multiculturalism*. Westport, CT: Praeger.

Schulz, K. (2016, August 15). The perilous lure of the Underground Railroad. *New Yorker*. Retrieved from https://www.newyorker.com/magazine/2016/08/22/the-perilous-lure-of-the-underground-railroad

Scranton, R. (2019, September 18). Narrative in the Anthropocene is the enemy: Stories won't save you from ecological destruction. *Literary Hub*. Retrieved from https://lithub.com/roy-scranton-narrative-in-the-anthropocene-is-the-enemy/?fbclid=IwAR1nZz7QI160XzIDT-PPmhhY5cXtIYxf6iajdR4ADgB3cc0Y_zZrf48wDMI

Shepherd, G. (1993). Building a discipline of communication. *Journal of Communication, 43(3)*, 83–91. https://doi.org/10.1111/j.1460-2466.1993.tb01279.x

Six Chinese cities with the best feng shui. (2013, May 30). Retrieved from http://en.people.cn/90782/8262134.html

Smith, R. E. (2001). *Principles of human communication*. Dubuque, IA: Kendall/Hunt.

Social Issues Research Center. (2004). The flirting report. Retrieved from http://www.sirc.org/publik/Flirt2.pdf

Sousa, L. (2012). Knowledge, truth, and the thing-in-itself. In J. Constancio & M. J. Mayer Branco (Eds.), *As the spider spins: Essays on Nietzsche's critique and use of language* (pp. 39–62). Berlin, Germany: De Gruyter.

Southwick, S. M., & Charney, D. S. (2018). *Resilience: The science of mastering life's greatest challenges*. New York, NY: Cambridge University Press.

Steinberg, S. (2006). *Introduction to communication*. Cape Town, South Africa: Juta.

Strate, L. (2008). Studying media as media: McLuhan and the media ecology approach. *Media Tropes Journal, 1*, 127–42.

Sukonik, M. (2016). *Letting go*. Unpublished paper.

Tannen, D. (1990). *You just don't understand: Women and men in conversation*. New York, NY: William Morrow and Company.

Tappin, B., van der Leer, L., & McKay, R. (2017, May 27). You're not going to change your mind. *New York Times*. Retrieved from https://www.nytimes.com/2017/05/27/opinion/sunday/youre-not-going-to-change-your-mind.html

Taub, A., & Nyhan, B. (2017, March 22). Why people continue to believe objectively false things. *New York Times*. Retrieved from https://www.nytimes.com/2017/03/22/upshot/why-objectively-false-things-continue-to-be-believed.html

Taylor, C. (2016). *The language animal: The full shape of the human linguistic capacity*. Cambridge, MA: Harvard University Press.

Thayer, L. (1974). Editor's introduction. *Communication, 1*, 1–4.

Thayer, L. (1983). "Realizing": Observations on the anti-philosophical state of the study of communication in Anglo-America. *Communication, 7*, 135–49.

Thayer, L. (2009). *Communication! A radically new approach to life's most perplexing problem*. New York, NY: Xlibris.

Thayer, L. (2011). *Explaining things: Inventing ourselves and our worlds*. New York, NY: Xlibris.

Trenholm, S. (1990). *Human communication theory*. Upper Saddle River, NJ: Prentice Hall.

Trivers, R. (2011). *The folly of fools: The logic of deceit and self-deception in human life*. New York, NY: Basic Books.

Twenge, J. M. (2017). *iGen: Why today's super-connected kids are growing up less rebellious, more tolerant, less happy—and completely unprepared for adulthood*. New York, NY: Atria Books.

Vickers, G. (1984). *The Vickers papers* (Open System Group, Ed.). New York, NY: Harper & Row.

Vickers, G. (1987). *Policymaking, communication, and social learning: Essays of Sir Geoffrey Vickers*. New Brunswick, NJ: Transaction Books.

Volosinov, V. N. (1994). Language and ideology. In J. Maybin (Ed.), *Language and literacy in social practice* (pp. 44–57). Tonawanda, NY: Multilingual Press.

Waldron, J. (2012). *The harm in hate speech*. Cambridge, MA: Harvard University Press.

Warkentin, G. (2014). Dead metaphor or working model? "The Book" in Native America. In M. Cohen & J. Glover (Eds.), *Colonial mediascapes: Sensory worlds of the early Americas* (pp. 47–75). Lincoln, NB: University of Nebraska Press.

Wells, L. (1985). Misunderstandings of and among cultures: The effects of transubstantiative error. In D. Vails-Weber and J. Potts (Eds.), *Sunrise seminars* (pp. 51–57). Arlington, VA: NTL Institute.

Wesch, M. (2009). YouTube and you. *Explorations in Media Ecology*. Retrieved from https://krex.k-state.edu/dspace/bitstream/handle/2097/6302/WeschEME2009.pdf

West, R., & Turner, L. (2014). *Introducing communication theory: Analysis and application*. New York, NY: McGraw-Hill Education.

Whalen, D. J. (1996). *I see what you mean: Persuasive business communication*. Thousand Oaks, CA: Sage.

Whorf, B. (1956). *Language, thought, and reality: Selected writings of Benjamin Lee Whorf*. Cambridge, MA: MIT Press.

Wolf, E. (1993, November). The Tlingit basket as rhetorical alternative form. Paper presented at the Speech Communication Association, Chicago, Illinois.

Wood, J. T. (2016). *Interpersonal communication: Everyday encounters*. Boston, MA: Cengage Learning.

Wright, R. (1999, November 8). We invite the hostages to return. *New Yorker*, 38–47.

Zaremba, A. J. (2010). *Crisis communication: Theory and practice*. New York, NY: M. E. Sharpe.

INDEX

Glossary definitions are indicated by page numbers in boldface. Figures are indicated by the letter "f."